El Al Airlines
Israel's National Airline

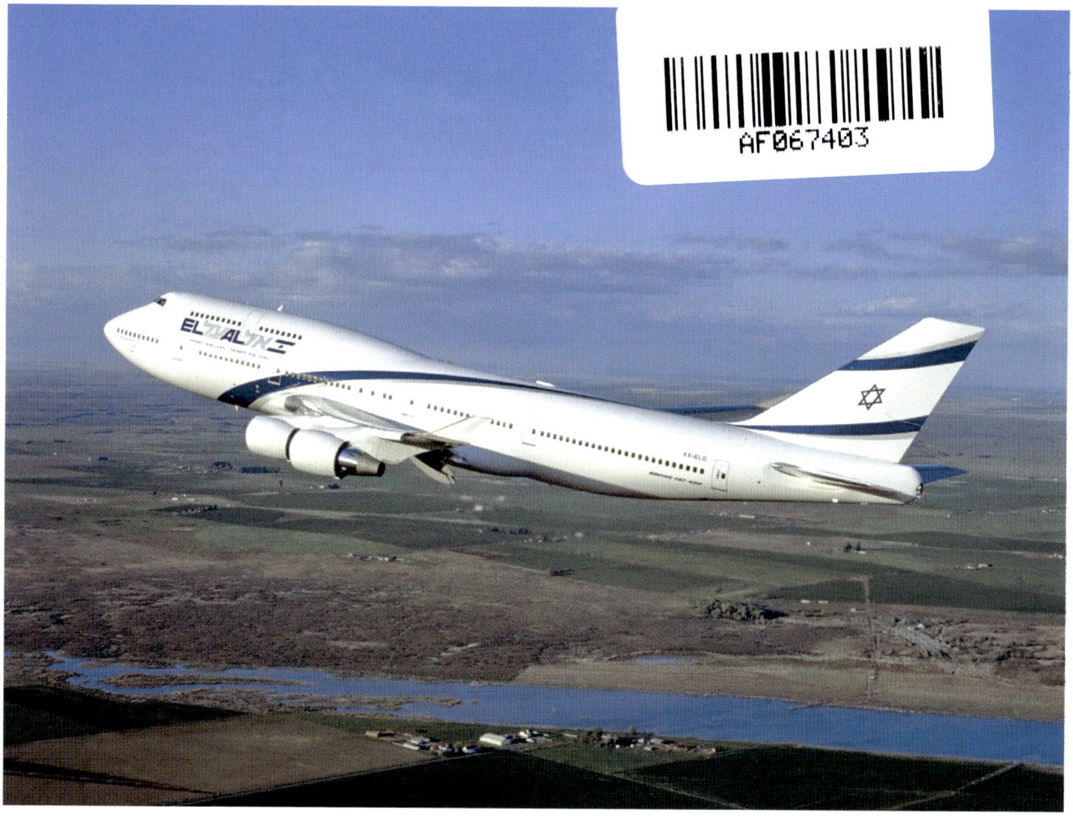

BABAK TAGHVAEE

KEY Books

AIRLINES SERIES, VOLUME 21

Front cover image: The backbone of El Al's wide-body and long-haul passenger aircraft fleet is four Boeing 787-858s including r/c 4X-ERC and 12 Boeing 787-958s. They connect Tel Aviv to various American and European destinations. (Babak Taghvaee)

Title page image: 4X-ELD, one of the four Boeing 747-458s that El Al operated until 2019, taken on 10 July 1999. Boeing 747-458s were the largest aircraft ever operated by El Al. They could carry a maximum of 403 passengers in three classes. (Israel Government Press Office)

Contents page image: El Al has operated at least 22 piston-engined aircraft including six Lockheed L-149 Constellations. This image, taken at Lod Airport, shows one of them on 1 April 1951. (Brauner Teddy / Israel Government Press Office)

Back cover image: This Boeing 737-804 with r/c 4X-EKM was used by the now defunct subsidiary Up by El Al between February and July 2014. It was painted in the airline's special livery and despite its return to El Al in July 2014, its livery remained unchanged for several months. (Babak Taghhvaee)

Published by Key Books
An imprint of Key Publishing Ltd
PO Box 100
Stamford
Lincs PE9 1XQ

www.keypublishing.com

The right of Babak Taghvaee to be identified as the author of this book has been asserted in accordance with the Copyright, Designs and Patents Act 1988 Sections 77 and 78.

Copyright © Babak Taghvaee, 2024

ISBN 978 1 80282 873 3

All rights reserved. Reproduction in whole or in part in any form whatsoever or by any means is strictly prohibited without the prior permission of the Publisher.

Typeset by SJmagic DESIGN SERVICES, India.

Contents

Introduction 4

Chapter 1 The Propliner Era 7

Chapter 2 The Narrow-Body Jetliners 27

Chapter 3 The Wide-Body Jetliners 60

Appendix 1 Incidents and Accidents 92

Appendix 2 El Al's Fleet Details 94

Introduction

Officially founded on 15 November 1948, El Al is Israel's flag carrier and the largest airline in Israel. It has a fleet of 46 passenger aircraft and one cargo aircraft. Among them, almost 40 have been simultaneously kept airworthy and ready for commercial use. While its fleet of 24 single-aisle narrow-body Boeing 737-858/958ERs connect Israel to many European destinations, the airline's twin-aisle wide-body and long-haul fleet of 16 Boeing 787-858/958s and six Boeing 777-228ERs connect Israel to long-distance destinations non-stop from Los Angeles in the US to Hong Kong in Southeast Asia.

El Al's foundation is deeply rooted in the history of Israel and its independence. The national airline of Israel was founded after a C-54B aircraft transported the president of Israel, Chaim Weizmann, from his temporary residence in Geneva, Switzerland, to Israel on 29 September 1948. A few weeks later, El Al was officially established with a base of C-54A/B Skymasters that were previously purchased by the Haganah Jewish paramilitary organisation. These aircraft had participated in several notable operations such as Operation *Balak*, to airlift arms and weapons to Israel from Czechoslovakia to be used by the Israeli Defence Force during the War of Independence in 1948.

El Al has owned and operated at least 22 piston-engined passenger aircraft, consisting of seven C-54A/Bs, eight C-46A/Ds, a C-47-DL, and six Lockheed Model 49-46/51 Constellations. The airline also operated five Bristol Model 175 Britannia turboprop-engined passenger aircraft before operating jetliners. Altogether, the airline has operated at least 101 different turbojet and turbofan-engined passenger aircraft in different variants, of those 76 were owned by the airline while the rest were operated under short- and long-term leasing contracts.

El Al's aircraft have been used for humanitarian relief and evacuation operations such as Operation *Magic Carpet* in which 47,000 Yemenite and 3,000 Habbani Jews were airlifted to Israel between June 1949 and September 1950; Operation *Ali Baba* (Ezra and Nehemiah) in which Iraqi Jewish and Christian immigrants were airlifted to Israel between May 1951 and January 1952; Operation *Exodus* to airlift hundreds of thousands of Soviet Jews to Israel in January 1990; and Operation *Solomon* to airlift 15,000 Ethiopian Jews to Israel in May 1991.

In June 2004, El Al offered stocks to the public. Privatisation of the airline commenced and was completed by 6 January 2005. This privatised airline has renovated its fleet of wide-body aircraft and its profitability has increased despite the impact of the ban on international air travel during the Covid-19 pandemic in 2020. The airline acquired four Boeing 787-858 and 12 Boeing 787-958 twin-engined wide-body airliners as replacements for its ageing but legendary Boeing 747-412/458, as well as its Boeing 767-300ER series twin-engined wide-body and long-haul airliners. These acquisitions significantly reduced the aircraft's operational costs per passenger on long-distance flights, particularly to the US, and subsequently increased profitability.

As of October 2023, when this book was written, El Al had 40 out of 46 passenger aircraft airworthy and was operating flights to Amsterdam, Athens, Bangkok, Barcelona, Boston, Budapest, Bucharest, Dubai, Dublin, Johannesburg, Larnaca, Lisbon, London, Los Angeles, Madrid, Marseille, Milan, Miami, Moscow, Munich, Naples, New York, Nice, Paris, Prague, Phuket, Rome, Sofia, Tbilisi, Thessaloniki, Tokyo, Venice, Vienna and Zürich. Some of the destinations including those to Sharm El Sheikh in Egypt

On 18 December 1934, the first purely commercial airline based in the UK's Mandate for Palestine was registered by Pinchas Rutenberg, the Jewish head of the electric company in Palestine, with funds from Jewish and British sources. The airline started its operations with two six-passenger Short S.16 Scions. VQ-PAB was one of them and is at Dov Hoz Airport located in north Tel Aviv. The Reading powerplant is in the background on 1 April 1938. (Israel Government Press Office)

Passengers on board a Scion passenger aircraft operated by Palestine Airways during a flight on 25 February 1939. Palestine Airways was the first Jewish airline in the history of Israel and was formed before the country gained independence. (Zoltan Kluger/Israel Government Press Office)

and Istanbul had temporarily stopped due to the increasing threats to Israeli nationals. Between 12 and 20 October 2023, El Al's aircraft were used to evacuate hundreds of Israeli citizens from Turkey, and were also chartered by the Israeli government to repatriate thousands of active duty and reservist personnel of the Israeli Defence Force who had participated in Operation *Iron Swords*, a response to the attack by Hamas, which killed 1,350 Israeli and other nationals around Gaza on 7 October 2023.

Today, El Al is one of the world's safest airlines. El Al protects its flights from hijackers and suicide bombers with extensive security screening and armed air marshals, and its aircraft are equipped with state-of-the-art, self-protection systems to protect from portable air-defence systems during take-off and landing, and also from surface-to-air and air-to-air missiles during flight.

Chapter 1
The Propliner Era

Douglas C-54 Skymaster: 1948–52

The Douglas DC-4 (C-54) Skymaster, a four-engined transport aircraft, was the first passenger aircraft used by El Al. The airline operated eight different examples comprising six C-54As and two C-54Bs. The 'B' variant had an increased fuel capacity in its wing, which resulted in an increase in the range of the aircraft. Capable of carrying a maximum of 44 passengers, the C-54A was used as a heavy-lift aircraft by the United States Army Air Force (USAAF) during World War Two. With its oversized cargo door, it had the capacity to load large cargo with a weight of 6,350kg (14,000lb).

In 1948, the Sherut Avir (Air Service) of Haganah (a Jewish paramilitary organisation), which later reorganised as an Air Transport Group, chartered a C-54A from an American company named Overseas Airlines. The aircraft was used to airlift weapons and ammunition from Zatec in Czechoslovakia to Beit Daras airfield in Israel during Operation *Balak*. The first flight of the chartered C-54A took place on the night of 31 March 1948, during which it airlifted 200 K-97 rifles, 40 machine guns and 150,000 bullets.

During the operation, about 100 round trips were conducted by three C-54s (one chartered and two owned), a single C-69 Constellation and 11 C-46A/D Commandos. During the operation, most of the flights were to Ekron Air Base (AB) near Tel Aviv, especially when the aircraft began airlifting Avia S-199 fighters, which Haganah procured in Czechoslovakia. While each C-46 could carry half an S-199 (two C-46s were needed to carry one S-199), one C-54A could carry a complete but disassembled S-199. S-199s were airlifted to Israel from Czechoslovakia's Zatec Air Base to Ekron Air Base from 20 May to 28 July 1948. The chartered C-54A was returned to its owner, and another C-54 was purchased for use in the operation.

In May 1948, the same day that David Ben-Gurion proclaimed Israel's independence, two C-54s purchased by Haganah joined its air service. The first aircraft was a C-54B-15-DO with construction number (c/n) 18395, which was delivered to the USAAF with serial number (s/n) 43-17195 on 21 November 1944. After World War Two, it was sold to US Overseas Airlines before its procurement by Haganah. It received s/n 1801 in Israel. The second aircraft was C-54A-15-DC with c/n 10348, which was delivered to the USAAF with s/n 42-72243 on 15 July 1944. It was sold to American Airlines in 1946 and was operated with registration code (r/c) NC90441 and fleet name *Flagship Rainbow One* before its procurement by Haganah. In Israel, it received s/n 1802.

After the establishment of the Israeli Air Force on 28 May 1948, both C-54s entered service with the Air Transport Group. The group was later reorganised as a Command, operating C-46A/D Commandos as well. The Command became No 106 Squadron based at Ekron Air Base. It was disbanded in 1949 and its C-54s were withdrawn and transferred to the newly formed Israeli airline El Al in 1948. Its C-46A/Ds were mostly absorbed by No 103 Squadron, an operator of C-47A/B Dakotas.

El Al's First Aircraft

On 18 August 1948, the Israeli Ministry of Transport, headed by David Remez, issued a document calling on the state to create an airline as a 'chosen instrument' for international civil aviation. This led to the official creation of El Al in November 1948. Before its official creation, 1801 and 1802 both received

El Al's markings and paint scheme and r/c 4X-ACA and 4X-ACB. These were the first civil registration codes issued for Israeli aircraft. Remez chose the name El Al after a biblical phrase meaning 'to the above or skies'.

The aircraft were used in late September to carry the newly designated first President of Israel, Chaim Weizmann, to Israel. For this purpose, 1801 was prepared as a civilian aircraft with r/c 4X-ACA (obtained on 27 September 1948) and owned by the airline. As no country was allowing the C-54B to land for refuelling, extra fuel tanks were added in Israel to enable it to fly to Geneva directly.

In service with the Israeli Air Force (IAF), 1801 and 1802 were used in two major operations before their transfer to El Al in November 1948. The first was *Balak* between 31 March and 12 August 12 1948; *Velvetta 1* provided navigational assistance for Spitfire IX fighters flying from Czechoslovakia to Israel between 24 and 27 September 1948; and also *Yoav* during the Arab-Israeli War in the Negev Desert in November 1948.

On 5 December 1948, 1802 was officially transferred to El Al and was operated by the airline until 22 February 1949 when it was sold. 1801, which had received r/c 4X-ACA was returned to the IAF and operated for arms transfer from Czechoslovakia to Israel. During Operation *Velvetta 2* in which Spitfire IXs were transferred to Israel, the aircraft developed engine problems and crashed on the beach at Tel Aviv while its crew were attempting to land on 2 June 1949. It was later scrapped after being declared unrepairable.

Following the sale of 4X-ACB to California Aircraft Corporation, its Israeli registration code was cancelled on 22 February 1949. The aircraft was operated in the US by Twentieth Century Aircraft and then Hemisphere Air Transport with American r/c N90441 while still owned by Jewish businessmen. In the months of its operations in the US, the aircraft passed an IRAN (Inspection and Repair if Necessary), which would not have been possible if it was still in use by El Al because of the US embargoes. The aircraft was transferred to Near East Air Transport and was leased to El Al for its flights to Europe in 1950.

As replacement for 4X-ACA and 4X-ACB, El Al obtained two other C-54s in 1949. The first was a C-54A-15-DC with c/n 10410, built for the USAAF in 1944, and operated by it as 42-7230 until 1946. El Al procured it via intermediary Flying Tiger Line. It was delivered to El Al at Tulsa, Oklahoma, on 15 March 1949, and arrived in Israel a few days later. It received r/c 4X-ACC with El Al and was named *Rechovoth* in honour of the city of President Chaim Weizmann's residence in Israel. The aircraft's time with El Al was short as it was sold to Flying Tiger Line in January 1952.

The next aircraft El Al procured, in 1949, was a 1944-built C-54A-10-DC, which had served with the USAAF until 1946. El Al used Flying Tiger Line to buy it. It was delivered to El Al in Tulsa on 26 February 1946 and arrived at Tel Aviv on 11 July 1949. The aircraft received r/c 4X-ACD. It was later named *Herzl* and was used in El Al's first scheduled flight from Tel Aviv to Rome and Paris. 4X-ACD was used to transport the remains of Theodor Herzl, the founder of Zionism from Tel Aviv to Vienna. The aircraft crashed during take-off from Tel Aviv at 0100hrs local time on 6 February 1950. The cause of the crash was ice formation caused by heavy snow. All of the crew and passengers survived but the aircraft was destroyed.

On 23 June 1950, a C-54B was used for the first time to fly from Tel Aviv to New York in a one-and-a-half-day-long journey. With seven crew members, 40 passengers and a parcel containing 37,000 letters, the aircraft flew to the US just four days after an agreement was signed between Israel and the US to establish passenger flights between the two countries. On its way from Lod to Idlewild Airport, New York, the aircraft had refuelling stops at Rome, Shannon, and Gander in Newfoundland, which increased the journey time to 40 hours.

Participation in Operation Ezra and Nehemiah

Several El Al C-54s participated in Operation *Ezra and Nehemiah* alongside several other El Al aircraft to evacuate 120,000–130,000 Iraqi Jews in 1951 and 1952. 4X-ACB, which had been transferred to Near East Air Transport, was one of two C-54As chartered by the Israeli government to evacuate the first 175 jews out of Iraq on 19 May 1950. As the Iraqi government intensified ethnic cleansing of Iraqi Jews, the Israeli government intensified evacuation flights, which led to launch of Operation *Ezra and Nehemiah*.

Before their participation in Operation *Ezra and Nehemiah*, El Al's C-54s also participated in Operation *Magic Carpet* to evacuate almost 47,000 Yemenite Jews and 3,000 Habbanim Jews from the Arabian Peninsula to Israel. The C-54s received the markings and registration codes of a Cuban airline named Intercontinental Aerea de Cuba during the operation.

In addition to the C-54A-15-DC with r/c 4X-ACC, El Al used three other Skymasters in Operation *Ezra and Nehemiah* comprising two C-54Bs with r/c 4X-ADB and 4X-ADC and a C-54A with r/c 4X-ADN. 4X-ADB, a C-54B-1-DC with c/n 10512, had been manufactured for the USAAF and had been operated by the force with s/n 42-72407 for a few months. El Al procured it by means of Flying Tiger Line on 27 April 1950. 4X-ADC was a C-54B-10-DO built in 1944 for the USAAF. It was operated by the force as 43-17167 until 1946. El Al procured it on 17 May 1950, while 4X-ADN, a C-54A-15-DC built in 1944 was operated by the USAAF as 42-72311 until 1945. 4X-ADN was purchased by the Israeli government to be operated by the IAF as a replacement for C-54A-15-DC with c/n 10348. It was transferred to El Al and operated as 4X-ACB in 1949. The C-54A-15-DC with c/n 10416 was transferred to El Al on 11 June 1950 and subsequently received r/c 4X-ADN.

4X-ACD was one of the Skymasters used by El Al. This C-54A-10-DC was operated by the Israeli Air Force before entering service with El Al. Named *Herzl*, the aircraft crashed during take-off from Tel Aviv on 6 February 1950. It is at Tel Aviv on 17 August 1949, when it repatriated the body of Theodor Herzl, founder of Zionism, to Israel. (Israel Government Press Office)

To participate in Operation *Ezra and Nehemiah*, El Al's C-46A/Ds and C-54A/Bs were painted with the colours and symbols of the American charter company Near East Air Transport (the same company that flew the Yemenite Jews in Operation *Magic Carpet*); the pilots were mostly El Al pilots with American passports (as required by the Iraqi authorities) and the destination of the flight was Nicosia in Cyprus. On 19 May 1950, a Skymaster plane took off with 86 immigrants accompanied by an Iraqi police officer. About two hours later, the plane landed at Nicosia Airport in Cyprus. A short time later, the plane took off again to Lod Airport, near Tel Aviv.

At the height of the operation, there were up to seven evacuation flights per day and there was an urgent need for additional planes and crews, beyond those provided by the Near East Air Transport company at the beginning. The workers of El Al's paint department, led by Meir Stein, worked hard to erase the El Al logo from the planes and to paint the American company logo over it. Later, the Israeli government chartered several C-54A/Bs from Alaska Airlines and the Cuban Intercontinental Aerea de Cuba.

El Al continued operating C-54A/Bs until the end of Operation *Ezra and Nehemiah*. Before the end of the Operation, 4X-ADN was sold to Trans-Caribbean Airways in June 1951. It crashed and burned during a cargo airlift flight while it was on descent into Zürich on 24 November 1951, resulting in the death of six of its crew, including pilot Captain Ted Gibson. One crew member survived. The airline's last Skymaster was 4X-ADC, which was sold to Flying Tiger Line on 7 April 1952, and was re-registered as N30058 on 25 April 1952. El Al fully replaced its Skymasters with Lockheed Constellations.

4X-ADC was a C-54B-10-DO operated by El Al between 1950 and 1952. It was built with s/n 43-17167 for the USAAF in 1944. It was delivered to the force on 25 September 1944. (Tony Clarke Collection via David Whitworth)

Another image of El Al's C-54B-10-DO with r/c 4X-ADC in Tel Aviv on 5 July 1950. (Katcoff Seymour/Israel Government Press Office)

4X-ACC, a Douglas C-54A-15-DC Skymaster at Lod Airport taken on 8 July 1951. A group of Reform Rabbis from the US arrived on a visit to Israel and can be seen next to the aircraft. (Teddy Brauner/Israel Government Press Office)

Curtis C-46 Commando: 1948–56

Relatively larger than the popular Douglas C-47 Dakota, the Curtis C-46 Commando transport aircraft had twice as much cargo volume and weighed almost twice as much as the C-47. Despite this, the C-46 was not as popular as the C-47, with around 3,000 constructed during World War Two, while 10,000 C-47s were built in total. The newly formed Israeli Air Force became one of the post-war operators of the C-46. The air force operated 14 different examples, which were in service with 106 Squadron; eight of them were transferred to El Al Israel Airlines.

C-46 Commandos played a vital role in airlifting during Operation *Balak*; they also led secondhand Spitfire IX fighters from Zatec to Israel during Operation *Velvetta*. During the War of Independence, in October 1948, they were used as high-altitude bombers at a time when the IAF lacked a sufficient number of heavy bombers (it had just three B-17Gs) to bomb Egyptian Army positions during Operation *Yoav*. During Operation *Avak*, the C-46A/Ds airlifted tons of military supplies for the Israeli Defence Force (IDF) troops in the Negev Desert preventing the Egyptian Army from besieging them in 1948 and 1949.

Through its history, El Al operated eight different Curtiss C-46 Commando aircraft for both passenger and cargo transport purposes. They were six C-46As and two C-46Ds, which had served with the Air Transport Group of the Haganah then Air Transport Command of the Israeli Air Force, and finally its 106 Squadron at Ekron. They were surviving examples of the 14 C-46A/Ds which had entered service with the air force thanks to Albert Schwimmer, the former TWA flight engineer and businessman living in New York who purchased them for Haganah, the Jewish paramilitary organisation which later became the Israeli Defence Force after Israel gained independence.

It is known that at least nine of the C-46A/Ds received s/n 1701 to 1709 in service with the IAF. Eight of them comprising six C-46As with s/n 1701, 1702, 1704, 1705, 1707 and 1708 and two C-46Ds with s/n 1703 and 1709.

In service with El Al, six C-46As were operated with their civil registration codes: 4X-ACF, 4X-AEF, 4X-ACT, 4X-ALA, 4X-ACE and 4X-ACG while the two C-46Ds were operated with their 4X-AQD and 4X-AQE registration codes. The first example to become operational with the airline was 4X-ACG/1708, which entered service on 22 January 1959. It was a C-46A-50-CU with c/n 40575. On 24 January 1950, three others entered service with El Al: 4X-ACE/1707, 4X-ACF/1701 and 4X-ACT/1404.

On 28 July 1950, two C-46Ds with r/c 4X-AQD and 4X-AQE (later they became 4X-ALE and 4X-ALF) entered service with El Al. C-46D was a paratroop transport variant of the C-46A fitted with an extra door on the port side. Out of the 3,181 C-46s built, 1,610 were this variant. Two years later, two more C-46As were delivered to El Al. They were C-46A-35-CU with r/c 4X-AEF (c/n 26802) and C-46A-36-CU with r/c 4X-ALA (c/n 26809), which had served with the IAF with s/n 1702 and 1705. They entered service on 12 March and 4 April 1952, respectively.

While El Al used ex-IAFs C-54s for high demand routes, the C-46s, each with 38 passenger seats, were used by the airline for the less travelled routes. Starting from 26 January 1950, El Al also dedicated two of its C-46s to freight operations between Israel and several European countries. The aircraft could export fresh Israeli products and other goods. From April 1951, one of the C-46s was used for weekly flights to London with stops in Athens, Rome, Düsseldorf and Amsterdam. Regular flights to Paris were also established later.

Before Israel gained its independence, Mossad Le Aliyah Bet, a branch of the Jewish paramilitary organisation Haganah in British Mandatory Palestine, secretly facilitated Jewish immigration to the area from various countries around the world. They chartered two C-46As as an airlift to transfer 100 Iraqi Jews from Baghdad to Israel. The aircraft were piloted by four non-Jewish American World War Two veteran pilots in April 1947.

Between May 1950 and December 1951, the state of Israel carried out Operation *Ali Baba* also known as *Ezra and Nehemia*. During the operation, more than 120,000 Jews were evacuated from Iraq via the Near East Transport company with help from El Al. The first planes flew to Israel via Cyprus. Several months later, a giant airlift operated directly from Baghdad to Lod Airport. As the Iraqi government had banned immigration to Israel, the aircraft airlifting the immigrants had to fly to Cyprus before taking the flight to Israel. Among the aircraft used in the operation, El Al's C-46As were present, and painted in the colours of the Near East Transport company. According to FAA regulations, they were allowed to carry a maximum 46 passengers; yet each airlifted 70 people per flight!

On 17 March 1949, C-46A-50-CU with r/c 4X-ACG crashed due to a portside engine failure upon landing at Sde Avraham Mar, an improvised landing strip about 55km (31 miles) north of Eilat. At the time of the incident, the aircraft was in use by the IAF during Operation *Uvda* (meaning Fact) to carry ammunition and fuel for Israeli troops that had advanced to Eilat and had taken control of it on 10 March 1949. The IAF occasionally operated other C-46s belonging to El Al during similar operations until 1952.

The remaining seven C-46s were in use with El Al for several more years until they were gradually withdrawn from service. C-46A-45-CU with c/n 30202 (4X-ACT which later became 4X-ALC) was transferred to Arkia, Israel's Inland Airlines on 28 February 1950. The other C-46s were sold to foreign customers. On 8 May 1953, 4X-AEF (c/n 26802) was sold, while two years later, El Al sold three others. They were 4X-ACE (sold 1 March 1955), 4X-ACF (sold 18 July 1955) and 4X-ALF (sold 18 July 1955). In January and February 1956, El Al's last two C-46s with r/c 4X-ALA and 4X-ALE were withdrawn from service.

This C-46A-55-CK with r/c 4X-ACF with s/n 1701, was the first of its kind to be operated by the Israeli Air Force between 1948 and 1950 when it was transferred to El Al. It was named *Eilana* (meaning Eilat) and was used during Operation *Ali Baba* to evacuate Iraqi refugees while carrying Cuban r/c CU-T-450. After the operation, it was re-registered, this time as 4X-ALB. (El Al's Archive)

Above: Arkia was founded as Israel's second airline. Also known as Israel Inland Air Service, Arkia was a subsidiary of El Al for years; El Al held 50 per cent of its shares. Arkia operated many of El Al's aircraft including this C-46A, which is carrying out a medical evacuation of Israeli government staff from Eilat to Tel Aviv in April 1951. (Fritz Cohen/Israel Government Press Office)

Left: 4X-ACT, which was later re-registered as 4X-ALC, was a C-46A-45-CU of El Al, which often flew to Eilat. It is behind one of the first El Al flight attendants during the first flight from Lod, Tel Aviv, to Eilat on 28 February 1950. (Teddy Brauner/Israel Government Press Office)

4X-ALC, which was previously 4X-ACT, was often used for flights to Eilat. It is at Eilat in January 1955. A group of tourists wait to board the aircraft. (Ilan Brauner/Israel Government Press Office)

Douglas C-47-DL Dakota: 1951–52

Douglas produced 10,174 examples of the Douglas DC-3 Dakota and its military version, the C-47 Skytrain, which was the most popular transport aircraft of World War Two. Despite carrying less cargo payload or passengers due to its relatively small size and less powerful engines, the C-47 was a more popular transport aircraft than the relatively larger and heavier Curtis C-46 Commando, even beyond World War Two. In service with the Israeli Air Force, the C-47s had a longer life than the C-46s, which were all withdrawn from service in the early 1950s.

The IAF received eight C-47A/Bs in 1948. Of these, three were lost in various incidents and accidents in that year and 1949. The IAF received seven more C-47s in 1950. Together with those delivered in 1948, they remained in service with the air force as transport and as special mission aircraft (signal intelligence gathering) until 2001. There is disagreement about the exact number of the C-47s that were with the IAF through its history; however, the exact number of civilian registration codes obtained for 34 of them from the Israeli civil aviation authority between 1948 and 1954 are known.

El Al operated only one of the Israeli Air Force's C-47s. The aircraft with c/n 6227 was a former USAAF C-47-DL with s/n 42-5639, which had been operated by the Royal Air Force with s/n FD773 during World War Two. On 12 November 1950, the aircraft entered service with the IAF and received s/n 1409 and r/c 4X-FAI. On 11 February 1951, it was transferred to El Al and received r/c 4X-ATA. It was then used for the inauguration of El Al's service from Tel Aviv to Istanbul via Nicosia on 1 March 1951.

The aircraft did not have a use in EL Al's service so was returned to the IAF on 25 January 1952, just 11 months after beginning operations with El Al. After five more years of military service, the aircraft with s/n 1409 was again found in civilian use, this time with Arkia Airlines from 2 April 1957 until 4 September 1968, when it was transferred to Israel Aircraft Industries.

This C-47-DL (DC-3C) with c/n 6227 was the sole example of its kind operated by El Al with r/c 4X-ATA and fleet name *Galilee*. It can be seen during the first flight of El Al to Eilat in 1951. (Israel Government Press Office)

Lockheed L-049/149 Constellation: 1950–62

El Al gradually replaced its Douglas C-54A/B Skymasters with Lockheed C-69 Constellations between 1950 and 1953. The C-69 is a military variant of the L-049. The Lockheed L-049 Constellation was the first model of the Lockheed Constellation family. The C-69 was a rival of the C-54 and subsequently, the civilian variants of these aircraft, the L-049 and DC-4 were also rivals. While the Skymasters were mostly manufactured for military customers, particularly the USAAF, the C-69 Constellation did not find success during World War Two. Only 22 examples were manufactured for the USAAF, while 1,170 of its rival, the C-54A/B/D/E/Gs, were manufactured for the USAAF, USN and then the USAF between 1942 and 1947.

After the war, an improved and stretched variant of the Lockheed L-049 named L-749 Super Constellation, was designed and manufactured and found wide use as a replacement for the C-54s in service with the USAF and USN. Mission variants of the aircraft, such as the EC-121 Warning Star airborne early warning and control radar surveillance aircraft, were produced between 1953 and 1958, which remained in use with the USAF and USN until 1978 and 1982, respectively.

Most of the C-69s were sold on the civilian market between 1946 and 1947, including four of the five Lockheed L-049s, which served with El Al. These four aircraft, which had r/c 4X-AKA to 4X-AKD in El Al's service were three C-69-1-LOs and one C-69-5-LO previously operated or ordered by the USAAF. The C-69-1-LOs with c/n 1965, 1967 and 1968 had s/n 43-10313, 43-10315 and 43-10316 during their short service in the USAAF, while the C-69-5-LO with c/n 1980 received s/n 42-94559 but was never taken up by the USAAF as World War Two ended just as it was completed.

The First Three Constellations

The three C-69-1-LOs were delivered to the USAAF on 25 January, 19 February and 11 May, respectively, while the C-69-5-LO was not taken up by the USAAF as the war had finished when it was completed. The three C-69-1-LOs became surplus and were retained at Burbank, California, for disposal by the US War Assets Administration, while the C-69-5-LO, which had been completed in 1946 was immediately demilitarised by Lockheed Aircraft Service (LAS) at New York, and sold to the British Overseas Airways Corporation.

On the request of Haganah, Albert Schwimmer (founder of Israel Aerospace Industries) purchased the three C-69-1-LOs through his airline and had them converted to Lockheed Model-49-46-10 civilian aircraft for future use by the Panamanian LAPSA. To transfer them to Israel, they received Panamanian registration codes RX-123, RX-124 and RX-121 respectively. Only the L-049 with c/n 1968 reached Israel. It left Burbank for Millville, New Jersey, on 26 January 1948, then flew to Tocumen Airport in Panama, via Newark, on 13 March. It then flew to Zatec (or Šatec) Air Base in Czechoslovakia with refuelling stops at Paramaribo in Suriname, Dakar in Senegal, and Casablanca in Morocco, between 19 and 21 June 1948.

The second and third L-049s left Burbank for Millville on 10 March 1948, and were impounded by the Federal Bureau of Investigation (FBI) as an illegal export from the US to Israel on 11 March 1948. They were stored at the airport until Schwimmer Aviation had them both released and flown to Burbank. While the L-049 that managed to reach Israel in June was used by Haganah's air service and then the Israeli Air Force to airlift weapons from Czechoslovakia to Israel during Operation *Balak*, the two remaining L-049s arrived in Israel and joined El Al directly in 1950.

Before their deliveries to El Al, they were converted to Lockheed Model L-149s. They were registered as 4X-AKA and 4X-AKB on 5 October 1950. 4X-AKA arrived in Israel on 25 March 1951, while 4X-AKB, named *Mazal Tov* (meaning good luck) arrived on 5 October 1950. El Al operated both until 1959 when they were offered for sale to Transazur Airlines, Switzerland, but without success. They remained stored at Lod until January 1962 when their registration codes were cancelled due to their sale to Universal Sky

Tours, UK. They were operated in the UK with r/c G-ARXE and G-ARVP until they were withdrawn from service at Luton in early 1965 and scrapped.

The sole L-049 in use with IAF during Operation *Balak* was damaged due to a wheels-up landing at Šatec Air Base caused by a hydraulic system failure on 13 July 1948. It was later withdrawn from the IAF's service. The aircraft was operated with a Panamanian r/c RX-121 during the Operation despite having s/n 2401 allocated to it by the IAF (although this was never applied on the aircraft). Albert Schwimmer obtained the aircraft, had it repaired and overhauled and then flown to Burbank in the US. It later joined Schwimmer's Intercontinental Airways. In April 1951, El Al purchased it and operated it with r/c 4X-AKC, which was issued by the Israeli civil aviation authority on 15 July 1951. 4X-AKC arrived at Lod Airport on 8 August 1951 and was quickly put into operations for European flights previously flown by the Skymasters.

4X-AKC was lost during El Al flight 402 from Tel Aviv to London via Vienna on 27 July 1955. The aircraft was shot down by two Bulgarian Air Force MiG-15 fighter jets (flown from Dobroslavtsi Airport) over Bulgaria, a few miles from the Greek-Bulgarian border. All seven crew and 51 passengers were killed. The incident took place during the Cold War, with each side interpreting the other's actions as serious provocation. The Bulgarian Communist government saw the incident as eroding the détente in East-West relations which were achieved in talks in Geneva earlier the same year.

Both MiG-15 pilots, Petrov (pair leader) and Sankiisky were considered for demotion and threatened with prison terms by the Minister of the Interior Georgi Tzankov but the pilots were found to have been following orders of the Chief of Air Defense, General Velitchko Georgiev. Although the Bulgarian government at first refused to accept responsibility, instead blaming the Israeli airliner for penetrating its airspace without authorisation, it eventually issued a formal apology stating that the fighter pilots had been 'too hasty' in shooting down the airliner and agreed to pay compensation to the victims' families.

Final Years of Constellation Operations

The fourth Constellation of El Al, was an ex-USAAF C-69-5-LO with c/n 1980, which was purchased by the airline directly in October 1953. Before its procurement, the aircraft had been rebuilt for leasing to California Hawaiian Airlines in April 1952. It arrived in Israel on 18 December 1953 and received r/c 4X-AKD on 24 December 1953. El Al operated it until February 1959 when it was proposed for sale to Trans Azur Airlines, Switzerland, as HB-IED but was not taken up. It was stored at Lod with 26,700 flying hours on its airframe until it was finally sold to Sky Tours, UK, in March 1962. The aircraft received r/c G-AHEN in the UK and was later transferred to Euravia Ltd, in May 1963, and was operated by that company until its retirement in early 1965, at Luton, where it was scrapped.

The fifth Constellation operated by El Al was L-049-51-26 with c/n 2061, which had been manufactured by Lockheed for Pan American in 1946. El Al purchased it in October 1955 and had it delivered in December of that year. It received r/c 4X-AKE in Israel and was put into service from February 1956. It was operated by El Al for just three years until February 1959 when it was proposed for sale to Trans Azur Airlines, Switzerland, as HB-IEC, but was not taken up. It then remained stored at Lod until 6 February 1962 when it was transferred to Israel Aircraft Industries and remained stored in its premises until 1965 when it was moved outside the airport for use as a restaurant next to Avia Hotel, but was finally scrapped.

The sixth and last Constellation that El Al owned and operated was registered as 4X-AOK. It was a L-049-46-21 built and delivered to Pan American as that airline's first Constellation on 3 February 1946. After service with Pan American, it was transferred to Cubana de Aviación (owned by Pan Am since 1932) in 1953, and re-registered as CU-T-547. It was purchased by El Al two years later and operated with r/c 4X-AOK in Israel. Its r/c was changed to 4X-AKE after another Constellation with the same r/c was retired and de-registered in 1962. There is little information about its operations with El Al but the aircraft was most likely not airworthy when it was withdrawn from use by El Al in 1968.

In addition to operating the six Constellations between 1949 and 1962, the airline also chartered or leased at least two L-749A Constellations from South African Airways between October and December 1955, and at least three L-1049 Super Constellations from KLM in 1961 and 1962, for flights between Tel Aviv and Johannesburg.

4X-AKC was built as a Lockheed Model 49-46-10/C-69-1-LO but was converted to a Model 149 after its procurement by El Al in April 1951. After the conversion, the aircraft arrived in Israel on 8 August 1951. It was shot down by MiG-15 fighter jets from the Bulgarian Air Force while it was on a scheduled flight from London to Tel Aviv via Vienna on 27 July 1955. This image shows it at Heathrow Airport on 6 April 1953. (Tony Clarke Collection via David Whitworth)

4X-AKB was a Model 49-46-10/C-69-1-LO, which El Al purchased in 1950. It arrived in Israel on 22 December 1950 and was named *Mazal Tov*. It was converted to a Model 049D to have a higher maximum take-off weight. In El Al's documentation, it was known as Lockheed Model 249. El Al sold it in January 1962. (David Eldan/Israel Government Press Office)

The first El Al Constellation with r/c N90827 during a test flight over Santa Monica Mountains, California, before its delivery in March 1951. This was built as Model 49-46-10/C-69-1-LO in 1944, and was delivered to the USAAF on 25 January 1945, but it was stored and later purchased by Haganah via Albert Schwimmer. It was converted to a Model 149 by Lockheed for El Al in 1951. (David Eldan/Israel Government Press Office)

4X-AKB was the second El Al Lockheed Model 049D. It is photographed at Lod Airport on the day it arrived, 22 December 1950. (Teddy Brauner/Israel Government Press Office)

Photographed in April 1951 is 4X-AKA, the first Lockheed Model 049D Constellation operated by El Al. It is refuelling at Lod Airport. (Teddy Brauner/Israel Government Press Office)

This image shows 4X-AKC, the third Constellation of El Al, at Lod Airport on 25 September 1951. New York's Mayor Impellitteri and his wife flew in this aircraft to Lod Airport. (Israel Government Press Office)

David Ben-Gurion and his wife in front of 4X-AKA after returning from the US. Ben-Gurion's young grandchild is running towards him at Lod Airport, Tel Aviv, on 7 May 1951. (Israel Government Press Office)

Bristol 175 Britannia: 1957–67

In the years between 1957 and 1967, El Al operated five different Bristol 175 turboprop-engined long-range passenger aircraft. The aircraft were used as a replacement for Lockheed L-149 (previously L-049) piston-engined long-range passenger aircraft to connect Israel to Asian and European destinations as well as the US. Designed and built by Bristol Aeroplane Company, this British passenger aircraft was one of the last turboprop engine airliners used for transatlantic flights.

The Series 310 aircraft, which had strengthened fuselage skin and an undercarriage with enhanced fuel capacity, was a long-range variant of the aircraft. It was ordered by the Israeli government for El Al. With a range of nearly 6,900km (4,300 miles) with maximum payload, and a cruising speed of 640km/h (400mph) at an altitude of 7,900m (26,000ft), the aircraft could perform transatlantic flights. Four were built for El Al with Series 313 designation.

In July 1958, El Al leased Bristol 175 Series 307F; it was previously ordered by BOAC and intended for use by British United Airways as a passenger aircraft. It was delivered to El Al with r/c 4X-AGE. El Al operated it as a stopgap solution for the fourth Series 313 until the newer series was ready. The aircraft returned to the Bristol Aeroplane Company in March 1959.

The Bristol Model 175 Series 310 had a price tag of US$4.5m (equivalent to US$40m today) per airframe, which was four to five times the price of a secondhand Lockheed Constellation. El Al's decision to procure four Series 310 models was announced on 17 March 1955 and subsequently, US$18m was invested for them to be used for transatlantic flights from 1957. On 22 June 1955, an order for three aircraft with an option for the fourth was finalised making El Al the first non-British buyer of the aircraft. This order was almost cancelled by Israeli officials when in July 1955, an El Al Constellation was mistakenly shot down by the Bulgarian Air Force. Efraim Ben-Arzi, president of El Al in 1956, saved the deal and made El Al an operator of the Bristol 175 Britannia.

El Al later increased its order from three to four. After months of delays, the first Britannia with Series 313 designation was ready on 5 September 1957 and one week later was flown from Filton, Bristol, to Tel Aviv. It was a non-stop flight lasting almost six hours as the aircraft's average speed was 645km/h (400mph) and the distance was 3,860km (2,400 miles). The first aircraft with c/n 13232 received Israeli r/c 4X-AGA and while it was in use for training with the second group of El Al Britannia pilots it was damaged in its rear fuselage section in Tel Aviv on 10 November 1957. It was flown to the UK for repairs and returned to Israel on 1 December 1957.

The remaining three Bristol 175 Series 313s with c/n 13233, 13234 and 13431, first flew at Filton on 2 September 1957, 4 October 1957 and 21 February 1959 with r/c 4X-AGB, 4X-AGC and 4X-AGD, respectively. They were handed over to El Al at Filton on 19 October 1957, 28 November 1957 and 7 March 1959, respectively.

Equipped with four Bristol Proteus 765 turboprop engines with 4,450shp (3,320kW) each for four-bladed propellers, the aircraft could carry 90 passengers in a two-class cabin configuration (18 business class and 72 tourist class). For the first time, on 18 and 19 December 1957, 4X-AGC under the control of El Al's Captain Zvi Tohar and Captain Danny Rosin performed a non-stop 9,800km (6,100 mile) flight in 14 hours and 56 minutes making it the longest non-stop flight performed by an airliner at that time. The fourth Britannia, which was modified during manufacture to nearly Series 320 standard, was used for the inauguration service to Tehran, Iran; the lone ally of Israel in the Middle East.

4X-AGB was an El Al Bristol 175 Britannia operated by the airline from 1957 until 1967, when it was sold. This image shows it landing at Heathrow in 1958. (Tony Clarke Collection via David Whitworth)

As El Al used Britannias for transatlantic flights, the remaining Constellations were removed from that service and were used for flights to European destinations. With the delivery of the fourth Britannia, the remaining Constellations were retired in 1959 and 1960. They were placed in storage and later sold to British buyers.

In 1960, 4X-AGD participated in a famous Mossad (Israel's secret service) operation named Operation *Eichmann*. Adolf Eichmann, a Nazi official living in Buenos Aires, Argentina, was involved in providing logistics for Nazi Germany. Under his command, trains and trucks were used to transport people to death camps.

Mossad found and arrested him in a complex operation. To secretly transfer him to Israel, President Ben-Arzi and Vice-President Ben-Ari negotiated with Argentine authorities to obtain a permit to fly 4X-AGD to Argentina. Eichmann was captured on 11 May 1960 and transferred to Israel by Mossad agents. In court he was charged with crimes against humanity and war crimes and was sentenced to death.

Transatlantic operations of El Al's Britannias ended after El Al began operating Boeing 707-420 Intercontinental passenger aircraft from January 1961. Thanks to their turbojet engines, they were faster, thus shortening the flight time from Tel Aviv to New York. The Britannias were subsequently dedicated to flights to European destinations and Iran until the last one was sold in February 1967.

4X-AGA was retired and sold to Globe-Air, Switzerland, on 3 April 1964. Before its withdrawal from service, it had been leased by El Al to British United Airways to be operated on behalf of El Al with r/c G-ASGV between 17 March and 1 April 1963. 4X-AGB, 4X-AGC and 4X-AGD were also leased to British United Airways and were temporarily operated by the airline for El Al with British r/cs G-ARWZ, G-ARXA and G-ASFU in 1962 and 1963. After their return to El Al and obtaining their Israeli r/cs again, they remained in service until they were sold to Globe-Air, Switzerland on 8 March 1965, British Eagle International Airlines on 19 April 1966, and Air Spain in February 1967 (4X-AGB).

4X-AGB was displayed during the SBAC Show at Farnborough, in September 1957, before its handover to El Al at Filton, Bristol, on 19 October that year. (John Read via Andrew Read)

This image shows a guard of honour at the farewell ceremony for President Yitzhak Ben Zvi and his entourage at the airport in Lod, before they left for a state visit to the Netherlands and Belgium on 14 July 1958. They flew in a Bristol Model 175 Britannia with r/c 4X-AGB for this trip. (Moshe Pridan/Israel Government Press Office)

The third El Al Bristol Model 175 Britannia with r/c 4X-AGC operated between 1957 and 1967. (Fritz Cohen/Israel Government Press Office)

The Israeli Postal Service loads parcels on board 4X-AGC at Lod Airport in March 1958. (Israel Government Press Office)

Chapter 2
The Narrow-Body Jetliners

Boeing 707-458: 1961–86

The Boeing 707 may be considered the world's first popular narrow-body passenger jetliner. The four-engined aircraft was built with many variants and entered service with many airlines in the 1950s. In 1957, when El Al began operating its first turboprop-engined Bristol Model 175 Britannia, studies for the procurement of a jet-engined passenger aircraft began. El Al representatives headed by Col Shlomo Lahat, its new vice president at that time, travelled to the US and visited aircraft factories to evaluate the Boeing 707, Convair 880/990 and Douglas DC-8.

The Intercontinental models of Boeing 707 powered by the new (at that time) Rolls-Royce turbofan engines, designated as Boeing Model 707-420 were selected. This model could fly 50 per cent faster than the already operational Britannias thanks to their maximum cruise speed of 965km/h (600mph). They could also carry larger payloads to longer destinations. With a maximum payload of 28,850kg (57,000lb), a Boeing Model 707-420 could fly for 9,260km (5,754 miles).

Subsequently, three Boeing 707-420s were ordered by El Al. Each was equipped with four Rolls-Royce Conway 508 (RCo.12) turbofans (or by-pass turbojets as Rolls-Royce called them) of 18,000lbf (80kN) thrust each. These engines had more thrust compared to the JT4A-3 or JT4A-5 turbojets, producing 15,800lbf (70kN) each on the Boeing 707-320. They were also more fuel efficient. The aircraft manufactured for El Al received a special name designation, which was Boeing 707-458.

The first two aircraft were ordered on 25 March 1960 and the third was ordered in February 1961. They had c/n 18070, 18071 and 18357 and received r/c 4X-ATA, 4X-ATB and 4X-ATC, and were delivered to El Al on 22 April 1961, 7 June 1961 and 13 February 1962, respectively.

Before receiving its first Boeing 707-458, a Boeing 707-441 (Model 707-420) owned by Brazilian Varig airline was leased by El Al for weekly flights from Tel-Aviv to New York until the first Boeing 707-458 was going to be ready. The Boeing 707-441 with r/c PP-VJB was used by El Al from December 1960 until June 1961. It flew to New York once a week from 9 January 1961, and then twice a week from 19 February 1961. Finally on 15 June 1961, 4X-ATA was used by El Al for a flight to New York. The aircraft had 97 passengers on board and was piloted by captains Tom Jones and Danny Rosin. The duration was 9 hours and 33 minutes.

Initially, Boeing 707-458s carried 115 passengers and no freight but this was later increased to 158 passengers for European flights and 120 passengers for flights to and from New York, but still without heavy cargo. The Britannias were removed from the Tel-Aviv–New York service after delivery of the Boeing 707s and were mostly used for flights to Europe and, occasionally, to Tehran. Thanks to their higher performance, including faster speed, El Al's Boeing 707s increased the frequency of transatlantic flights by 60 per cent.

As the number of these aircraft in El Al's service was limited, there was significant pressure on this small fleet to connect Israel to various countries around the world. By 1964, the Israel Aircraft Industries (IAI) gained all the necessary qualifications to perform all sorts of maintenance domestically at Lod or Ben

Gurion airports including depot maintenance or overhaul. However, the IAI was still unable to perform engine maintenance forcing El Al to obtain special pods for carrying the engines requiring maintenance under the wings of its aircraft during flights to London and Paris. The Rolls-Royce engines were overhauled in England while the Pratt & Whitney JT3D engines, which were later installed on El Al's Boeing 720Bs, were overhauled by SNECMA in France.

El Al's Boeing 707s were used to carry spare parts for the fighter jets of the Israeli Air Force including Dassault Mirage IIIs from France. This was intensified before the Six-Day War in June 1967. Before the start of the war on 5 June 1967, the scheduled flights of El Al for that day (three flights) departed Lod airport without any delay or problem. These three aircraft returned to the airport later in the final hours of 5 June. After the start of the war, the Jordanian Army was able to shell Lod Airport with 155mm artillery projectiles. Therefore, because of this threat, El Al had its passengers checked in before their flights in the Avia Hotel outside the airport. Finally, on the second day of the war, once the IAF established air superiority, these attacks were stopped and El Al resumed its normal flight activities.

A year after the Six-Day War, the Popular Front for the Liberation of Palestine (PFLP) targeted one of the three El Al Boeing 707-458s. The aircraft, with r/c 4X-ATA in use for flight LY426 from Rome's Fiumicino Airport to Tel Aviv's Lod Airport was hijacked by three members of the PFLP terrorist organisation. Armed with grenades and revolvers, they shot first officer Maoz Poraz, took control of the aircraft and forced its pilot to fly to Algiers. Terrorists later released the passengers under pressure from the Algerian authorities but kept the crew hostage. They later released the crew gradually until 1 September. Algeria released 4X-ATA, which was later flown by a French crew from Algiers to Rome where El Al took over and flew it back to Tel Aviv.

After two more terrorist attacks that targeted El Al's Boeing 707/720s, the airline employed security guards on board the aircraft to protect crew and passengers from terror threats. This was successful. On 6 September 1970, when an Arab terrorist named Leila Khaled (who had been involved in the TWAs hijacking in August 1969) and her male companion Patrick Argullo tried to use revolvers and grenades to hijack El Al Flight 219 with r/c 4X-ATB from Amsterdam to New York, an El Al air marshall confronted them.

Attempting to make their way into the cockpit, the hijackers took a flight attendant hostage, forced her to stand next to the cockpit door and demanded the pilots open the door. Pilots Captain Uri Bar-Lev and First Officer Arie Oz refused and, instead, they pushed the control yoke forward and made the 4X-ATB dive, which resulted in the terrorists jumping and hitting the roof of the cabin. After coming out of the dive, Argullo killed a flight attendant named Shlomo Vider but was then shot and killed by an El Al air guard. Leila Khaled was pinned down by a passenger and another flight attendant. The aircraft was diverted to London where it made an emergency landing. Khaled was arrested but was released later after PFLP hijacked a British passenger aircraft and took its passenger and crew hostage and had them exchanged for Khaled.

4X-ATA, 4X-ATB and 4X-ATC were later retired from El Al's service in March 1984, September 1986 and January 1980, respectively. Before its retirement, 4X-ATB was leased to Arkia between 4 April 1984 and 6 July 1986. It was later sold to Boeing, and received r/c N32824 and then r/c N130KR. The aircraft was donated to Lufthansa to mark nearly 30 years of its Boeing 707 operations during the handover ceremony of the 200th Boeing 737-300 to El Al on 21 November 1986 in Berlin, and was painted in Lufthansa colours. Lufthansa passed it to the Verkehr und Technik Museum, known today as the German Museum of Technology (Deutsches Technikmuseum).

The Boeing 707 with r/c 4X-ATB was kept on the premises of Israeli Aerospace Industries in Ben Gurion Airport until 20 November 1986 when it was flown to Frankfurt. A day later, Boeing received the aircraft, which by then had received r/c N130KR. It was delivered to Lufthansa at Berlin-Tegel airport.

4X-ATA was an El Al Boeing 707-458, which was operated by the airline between 1961 and 1984. It is landing at Heathrow Airport in 1962. (Tony Clarke Collection via David Whitworth)

This is the only remaining section of El Al's Boeing 707-458 with r/c 4X-ATA when it was on display at the USS Intrepid Museum in 1989. (Fergal Goodman)

El Al's Boeing 707-458 with r/c 4X-ATB at Heathrow Airport in July 1972. (Keld Bonfizz)

After several years on display in the colours of a former Lufthansa Boeing 707-430 with r/c D-ABOC, this ex-El Al Boeing 707-458 with r/c 4X-ATB was scrapped in May 1951 at Berlin Tegel Airport. (Dirk Grothe)

4X-ATC, the third El Al Boeing 707-458 is under routine maintenance in one of the hangars at Lod Airport in November 1966. (Fritz Cohen/Israel Government Press Office)

The aircraft was painted in the colours of Lufthansa's Boeing 707 with r/c D-ABOC but from 1998 until 10 May 2021 when it was scrapped, it remained abandoned.

4X-ATC was sold to Zaire Aero Service after retirement and was operated with r/c 9Q-CPM until it was delivered to Wolf Aviation where it received r/c 9Q-CWR in November 1983. It was damaged in a landing accident at Isiro, Zaire, in 1984, and was scrapped in Kinshasa in the Democratic Republic of the Congo in January 1986. 4X-ATA had accumulated 61,228 flying hours across 29,021 cycles at the time of its retirement and found no buyers so was scrapped at Ben Gurion Airport in July 1984. Its nose section was delivered to Intrepid Air and Sea Museum, which put it on display on aircraft carrier USS Intrepid in the Hudson, New York City, from April 1985 until April 2000, when the nose or cockpit section was moved to the Cradle of Aviation Museum in Mitchell Field, New York.

Boeing 707-358B/C: 1966–92

In 1962, Boeing developed one of the best variants of the Boeing 707 passenger aircraft. Known as Series 320B, it had more powerful and fuel-efficient Pratt & Whitney JT3D turbofan engines, a modified wing and a stronger structure to support a maximum take-off weight, which was increased by 8,600kg (19,000lb). The aircraft's maximum range was increased to enable non-stop flights from Europe to West Coast destinations in the US, as well as flights from the US to Japan.

El Al operated seven Israeli-registered Boeing Model 707-320Bs, including two 320C series sub-variants. Model 707-320C was a convertible variant of Model 707-320B with a large fuselage cargo door. It also had a revised wing with three-sectioned leading-edge flaps to improve take-off and landing performance and enabling the aircraft to have its ventral fin removed. The same wing of Model 707-320C was later incorporated into the Model 707-320Bs built after 1963. These aircraft, with the three-sectioned leading-edge flaps, became known as Boeing 707-320B Advanced.

El Al ordered three Boeing 707-320Bs and two Boeing 707-320Cs. They were built and delivered as Boeing 707-358B/Cs (the '58' digits were used by Boeing to refer to the aircraft built for El Al). The first two Boeing 707-358Bs were Advanced variants while the third was a heavy variant with new leading-edge flaps similar to model 707-320Cs. These aircraft, with c/n 19004, 19502 and 20097, were ordered in September 1964, July 1966 and October 1967, respectively. They received r/c 4X-ATR, 4X-ATS and 4X-ATT and took their first flights on 10 December 1965, 23 January 1967 and 15 January 1969. They were handed over to El Al a few days after their first flights.

The Model 707-320Cs, which were delivered as Boeing 707-358Cs, were 4X-ATX (c/n 20122) and 4X-ATY (c/n 20301). They were ordered in December 1967 and October 1968 respectively. They were rolled out of the factory on 2 April 1969 and 19 December 1969 and delivered to El Al on 15 May 1969 and 26 January 1970, respectively.

An El Al Boeing 707-358B with r/c 4X-ATR was attacked on 26 December 1968 when two Algerian terrorists entered the ramp of Athens airport. One had a sub-machine gun and used it to fire at the front section of the aircraft. One bullet pierced a window and killed a passenger instantly. Another terrorist threw a grenade into the number one engine. Greek police soon overpowered the terrorists and El Al passengers and crew were evacuated. PFLP later took responsibility for the attack. In response, the IDF attacked Beirut International Airport. IDF commandos used the IAF helicopters to fly to the airport and destroy 12 passenger aircraft of Arab airlines there.

During their career in El Al's service, the Boeing 707-358B/Cs were leased to other airlines for a short period of time. 4X-ATR was leased to Flying Tiger Line between 7 January and 3 October 1966. In this period, it was flown by this airline with r/c N317F and was once wet-leased (with crew) back to El Al. The same aircraft was also leased to El Al's subsidiary, the Sun d'Or in August 1981 and was used for flights to Düsseldorf and other European destinations until 1 May 1982, when it was returned to El Al. The aircraft was also leased to Arkia from 6 January 1987 to 14 April 1988.

4X-ATS, 4X-ATT and 4X-ATX were also leased to Arkia. The first was leased between 24 April 1987 and 7 October 1988; the second between 11 April and 31 May 1988; and the third between 12 October 1986 and 5 January 1987. 4X-ATY, the second Boeing 707-358C was leased to Sun d'Or between 1 May 1982 and 7 July 1986. Procurement of modern Boeing 757 narrow-body jetliners and Boeing 767 wide-body passenger aircraft and their deliveries between 1984 and 1987 allowed El Al to lease its Boeing 707s to Arkia and Sun d'Or until their retirement.

El Al retired its Boeing 707-358B/Cs between 1988 and 1992. 4X-ATR was retired after its last service from Madrid to Tel Aviv on 14 April 1988. It was sold to Jet Aviation Components & Aircraft just a few days later. 4X-ATS was sold to Israel Aircraft Industries on 29 January 1989. 4X-ATT was sold to Jet Aviation Components & Aircraft on 9 June 1988. 4X-ATX was sold to Israel Aircraft Industries on 20 July 1994, two years after its last service and retirement on 28 December 1992, while 4X-ATY was sold to World Jet Aircraft on 28 March 1991.

In 1982, El Al expanded its Boeing Model 707-320B/C fleet to six by means of procuring a Boeing 707-331B Advanced with c/n 18985 from Trans World Airlines. It received Israeli r/c 4X-ATD on 23 April 1982 and was delivered to El Al three days later. It entered service on 30 April 1982. El Al leased it to Arkia from 1 April 1985 to 29 January 1989. It was sold to Hartford Power Systems, Inc, by El Al on 26 January 1989.

From 17 July 1983, El Al sub-leased a Boeing 707-328B with c/n 18456 (built in 1962) from Air Supply Corp, which itself had leased it from Tratco, the owner. The aircraft received r/c 4X-ATE in El Al's service, which expired on 10 October 1983.

This image shows 4X-ATR, a Boeing 707-358B, which was operated by El Al between 1966 and 1988. The aircraft is in front of the terminal of Lod Airport in November 1966. (Fritz Cohen/Israel Government Press Office)

4X-ATS, an El Al Boeing 707-358B, is escorted by an M113 Swiss police armoured personnel carrier after landing in Zürich to protect it from the danger of Palestinian terrorists on 26 August 1984. (Lewis Grant)

A welcoming ceremony for Prime Minister Levi Eshkol and his wife Miriam at Lod Airport, after their return from a visit to the US, Canada and England on 18 January 1968. They used Boeing 707-358B with r/c 4X-ATS for their trip. (Fritz Cohen/Israel Government Press Office)

4X-ATY, an El Al Boeing 707-358C departs Heathrow Airport in May 1981 when it was in use by the airline's subsidiary, Sun d'Or International Airlines. (Aero Icarus)

Boeing 707-441 with r/c PP-VJB was leased to El Al between December 1960 and May 1961. The airline also leased six other Boeing 707s, including two Boeing 707-349Cs with r/c N324F between April and August 1968 and r/c N325F August to December 1968 from Flying Tiger Line; a Boeing 707-321 with r/c G-AYBJ from British Midland Airways between August and September 1972; a Boeing 707-329 with r/c 4X-BYM from Israel Aircraft Industries in 1977; a Boeing 707-138B with r/c N792FA from F B Ayer & Associates via Israel Aircraft Industries between 13 March and 1 November 1978; and a Boeing 707-323B with r/c 4X-ATG from Arkia in 1990.

Boeing 720-058B: 1962–80

In July 1957, Boeing Commercial announced the development of a derivative of the Boeing 707 for shorter flights. The Boeing 720 prototype logged its maiden flight on 23 November 1959. Its type certificate was issued on 30 June 1960, and it entered service with United Airlines on 5 July 1960. A total of 154 Boeing 720s and 720Bs were built until 1967. As a derivative, the 720 had low development costs, allowing profitability despite few sales.

Compared to the Boeing 707-120, the shortest variant of the Boeing 707 family, the Boeing 720 was 2.54m (8 ⅓ft) shorter. It had a modified wing and a lightened airframe for a lower maximum take-off weight. The first Boeing 720s were equipped with Pratt & Whitney JT3C turbojets enabling them to transport 131 passengers, in two classes, to a maximum distance of 5,200km (2,800nmi/3,200 miles). The introduction of the JT3D turbofan powerplants enabled construction of the Boeing 720B, the first example of which flew for the first time on 6 October 1960 and entered service in March 1961. It could carry 156 passengers in one class to a maximum 5,900km (3,200nmi/3,700 miles).

El Al has operated two Boeing 720-058Bs with c/n 18424 and 18425, which were ordered on 3 May 1961. They received r/c 4X-ABA and 4X-ABB on 19 October 1961 and had logged their first flights on 16 March and 23 April 1962, respectively. The aircraft were delivered on 23 March and 30 April 1962, respectively. Procurement of these aircraft was directly related to the Arab boycott in which many Arab and anti-semite states in Africa and the Middle East closed their airspaces to Israeli aircraft from 1955, and as a consequence El Al had difficulty reaching Johannesburg, South Africa. For seven years, El Al had to charter aircraft from other airlines, which took a long route around North and West Africa to get to their destination. With the new Boeing 720-058Bs, the airline had no need to refuel in Tehran, and could fly its own aircraft direct.

On 14 June 1962, the Boeing 720-058Bs took over the service from Tel Aviv to Tehran. These flights were previously served by Bristol Model 175 Britannias, then Boeing 707s. Mehrabad International Airport was also used as a refuelling point to continue flights to Africa. After flying over Iran, the Gulf of Oman and the Indian Ocean, aircraft could fly to Nairobi and after refuelling there, continue on to Johannesburg. From summer 1962, Boeing 720-058Bs took over the European and short-distance flights from the last El Al Bristol Model 175 Britannias.

In 1965, El Al replaced its original Boeing 720-058Bs JT3D-1 turbofans with more powerful JT3D-3Bs. These engines were more powerful and fuel efficient and, being the same model used on the Boeing 707-358/Cs, helped reduce their maintenance costs as well as spare parts.

However, these Boeing 720-058Bs were also the target of terrorism. On 18 February 1969, El Al flight LY432 (a Boeing 720-058B with r/c 4X-ABB), carrying 11 crew and 17 passengers was attacked. The aircraft was taxiing on the runway of Zürich's Airport following a stopover from Amsterdam to Tel Aviv when it was attacked.

The terrorists were waiting near a fence at the edge of the runway. As 4X-ABB approached, they sprayed it with bullets from sub-machine guns and threw grenades at it. Almost 40 bullets pierced the cockpit and killed Yoral Peres, one of the pilots. Mordechai Rahamim, on board the aircraft, opened the

Boeing 720-058B with r/c 4X-ABA is taking off from Béziers Cap d'Agde Airport, near Languedoc, in 1975. (Keld Bonfizz)

Boeing 720-058B with r/c 4X-ABB is landing at Lod Airport on 23 February 1972. (Moshe Milner/Israel Government Press Office)

door and immediately started shooting back, killing one of the terrorists. He and the three terrorists were later arrested by Swiss police. PFLP took responsibility for the attack. Rahamim was released after it became known that he was a security guard on board the aircraft. The aircraft was repaired and returned to service six days later.

El Al continued to operate its Boeing 720-058Bs (also known as Boeing 720Bs) until 28 August 1980 when both were sold to Jet Power. At the time of the sale, 4X-ABA had accumulated 51,668 flying hours and 20,329 cycles, while 4X-ABB had accumulated 51,299 flying hours and 20,425 cycles. They received r/c N8498S and N4228G in the US. Boeing Military purchased them from their American operator on 2 August 1984 and 20 July 1983 respectively. Both were sent to Davis Monthan Air Force Base where they were put in storage and used for parts for the KC-135 Stratotanker. The first ex-El Al Boeing 720B was scrapped in 1985 while the latter was scrapped in 1991.

Boeing 737-258 Adv: 1980–2000

Following the sale of the two Boeing 720-058Bs in August 1980, El Al planned to purchase a pair of Boeing 737-200 series short-haul passenger aircraft as a replacement. Between the sale and purchase, the airline leased two Boeing 737-2M8(A) aircraft from TEA (Trans European Airways) in 1981. The aircraft, with c/n 21736 and 22090, had been built in 1979 and 1980, respectively, and were operational with TEA with r/c OO-TEL and OO-TEO from 1 March 1979 and 19 May 1980. El Al began dry leasing them in October 1981 until 30 June and 30 September 1982 respectively. They had r/c 4X-ABL and 4X-ABM when operated by El Al.

Two Boeing 737-258s with c/n 22856/910 and 22857/919 were delivered to El Al on 30 September and 9 November respectively. The aircraft received r/cs 4X-ABN and 4X-ABO. Each had a pair of JT8D-17A turbojet engines, which were more powerful than the JT8D-15 engines of the leased Boeing 737-2M8s.

Boeing 737-2M8 with r/c 4X-ABL (c/n 21736/557) was leased by El Al between 1981 and 1982. At that time, the aircraft was three years old and had previously been leased to Libyan Arab Airlines for two years. Photograph taken in March 1982. (Herwart Schneider via Stefan Röhrich)

The second Boeing 737-2M8 with r/c 4X-ABM (c/n 22090/664) was leased from TEA (Trans European Airways) between October 1981 and December 1982. (Kev Colbran)

Boeing 737-258 with r/c 4X-ABN is taking off from Frankfurt Airport in July 1991. (Keld Bonfizz)

Boeing 737-258 with r/c 4X-ABO at Munich Airport escorted by West German police in armoured personnel carriers on 5 August 1985. (Neil D Brant)

El Al also selected long-haul and wide-body Boeing 767s, ordering four of them with deliveries in 1983 and 1984. The two Boeing 767-258s had r/c 4X-EAA and 4X-EAB and two Boeing 767-258ER (Extended Range) had r/c 4X-EAC and 4X-EAD. Two Boeing 767-27EER variants were purchased and received in 1999. They received r/c 4X-EAE and 4X-EAF.

With 111 seats in a full economy class, the Boeing 737-258s were used on shorter routes to Europe, as well as on domestic flights from Ben Gurion Airport to Eilat during the tourist seasons. During their service with El Al, they were leased to Guiness Peat Aviation, which sub-leased them to LAN-Chile with r/c CC-CJK and CC-CJM from 10 March 1988 until December 1988. They were leased to Arkia from January 1989 until they were sold to Nationwide Air of South Africa. They received r/c ZS-OOC and ZS-OOD there.

Boeing 757-258: 1987–2012

The Boeing 707 narrow-body airliner was designed and built as a successor to the tri-engine Boeing 727. The aircraft, with its wide fuselage to accommodate six-abreast seating was widely acquired and used as a replacement for Boeing 707-300 series passenger aircraft by many airlines including El Al. The airline has operated 11 different Boeing 757-300 series aircraft; among them, seven were owned by the airline while four others had been dry-leased. In addition, El Al wet-leased two other Boeing 757s for a short time.

In October 1986, El Al ordered three Boeing 757-200 series aircraft as a replacement for its ageing Boeing 707s for flights to European destinations where noise limitations were in place. The aircraft were designated as Boeing 757-258s and received Rolls-Royce RB211-535E4 turbofan engines that burned nearly 50 per cent less fuel than the four Pratt & Whitney JT3D-3s of El Al's Boeing 707s. The Boeing 757s were delivered from 1987, enabling El Al to remove its Boeing 707s from commercial service in 1989, leaving just two examples in operation. 4X-ATX, which was leased to Arkia and then Sun d'Or for passenger charter flights to Europe, and 4X-ATY, which was used for cargo flights. These two aircraft had their engines modified and equipped with hush kits to reduce their noise and allow them to operate in every European country.

The three new Boeing 757-258s were 4X-EBL, 4X-EBM and 4X-EBR with c/n 23917/152, 23918/156 and 24245/174. They rolled out of the factory on 23 October 1987, 8 November 1987 and 10 June 1988 and were delivered to El Al on 25 November 1987, 17 December 1987 and 19 July 1988. They received fleet numbers 501 to 503. 4X-EBL flew a commercial flight on 10 December 1987 from Tel Aviv to Brussels. The other two logged their commercial flights on 20 December 1987 and 20 July 1988 respectively.

4X-EBL was the first Boeing 757-258 that El Al operated between 1987 and 2000. It is in Zürich and being escorted by Swiss police in March 1988. (Aero Icarus)

El Al purchased four more Boeing 757s in 1990, which were all extended transcontinental (ET) variants suitable for long-range flights. The aircraft with c/n 24884, 25036, 26053 and 26054 were rolled out of the final assembly line on 2 October 1990, 21 February 1991, 29 January 1993 and 19 April 1993 respectively. They received r/c 4X-EBS, 4X-EBT, 4X-EBU and 4X-EBV, respectively and their deliveries took place on 13 November 1990, 1 April 1991, 8 March 1993 and 5 May 1993, respectively.

The three Boeing 757-258s and four Boeing 757-258ETs were leased to various airlines while they were with El Al. 4X-EBL, 4X-EBM and 4X-EBS were leased to Arkia several times. At the end of their

career, 4X-EBM, 4X-EBO, 4X-EBS, 4X-EBT and 4X-EBY (sub-leased) were operated by Sun d'Or (El Al's subsidiary). 4X-EBM and 4X-EBI were leased and sub-leased to Israir Airlines.

In addition to the seven Boeing 757-258s owned by El Al, an eighth aircraft of the extended transcontinental variant with r/c 4X-EBI and c/n 27622 was acquired under a long-term leasing contract with International Lease Finance Corp (ILFC). The aircraft had rolled out of the factory on 18 February 1997 and was leased to El Al from 24 March 1997 until March 2007. It was sub-leased to Israir on 5 July 2002.

Three other Boeing 757s, which were leased by El Al for a long time and received Israeli r/cs were two Boeing 757-27Bs with c/n 24136 and 24137 and El Al r/c 4X-EBF and 4X-EBY. The former was operated by El Al from 15 May 1996 to 17 April 2000 and the latter from 18 February 1994 to October 2007. The third leased aircraft, which received an Israeli r/c was a Boeing 757-236(ET) with c/n 24120, which was dry-leased from Haifa LLC by El Al from 15 April 2003 to 27 February 2007. It was operated with r/c 4X-EBO during its service with the airline.

For a short time, El Al also wet-leased or chartered two other Boeing 757s, which were G-BPEA and N757NA. The former, a Boeing 757-236, was leased from British Airways from 18 March 1990 and 1 May 1990 while the latter, which was a North American Airlines Boeing 757-32A, was chartered in March 1990. The Boeing 757-258s leased to Arkia had full economy class cabin seating for 215 passengers while the others had cabin seating for 178 passengers (16 business and 162 economy).

As a replacement for its Boeing 757s, El Al procured Boeing 737-858s and Boeing 737-958ERs. The seven Boeing 757s with r/c 4X-EBL, 4X-EBM, 4X-EBR, 4X-EBS, 4X-EBT, 4X-EBU and 4X-EBV were withdrawn from use or sold on 23 May 2000, 11 November 2011, 4 October 1991, 6 May 2011, 22 February 2012, 27 November 2012 and 26 November 2012. 4X-EBI, which had been leased from ILFC, was returned to its lessor in March 2007.

El Al operated 4X-EBS, a Boeing 757-258(ET) between 1990 and 2011. This aircraft is at Geneva on 25 March 2007. (Aero Icarus)

El Al's Boeing 757-258(ET) with r/c 4X-EBT in Zürich on 11 August 2000. (Aero Icarus)

Boeing 757-258(ET) with r/c 4X-EBU, on 12 June 2011, in its new colours just a year before its retirement from El Al's service. (Aero Icarus)

4X-EBV, an El Al Boeing 757-258(ET) landing at Zürich on 22 August 2008. (Aero Icarus)

Sun d'Or, the subsidiary of El Al, operated this Boeing 757-236(ET) between 2003 and 2007. It is at Geneva in the colours of Sun d'Or on 28 January 2006. (Keld Bonfizz)

El Al had this Boeing 757-27B(ET) transferred to Sun d'Or in 2004 until 2007. It is at Geneva on 29 January 2005. (Keld Bonfizz)

Boeing 737-758/858: 1999–Today

As the age, flying hours and cycles of El Al's Boeing 757s increased in the 1990s, the airline started planning to replace them with Boeing's Next Generation 737s. At the same time, the airline began searching for a replacement for its two Boeing 737-258s with r/c 4X-ABL and 4X-ABM, which were in service from 1981. The airline evaluated Airbus' A319 and Boeing's 737-700 series as a replacement for Boeing's 737-258s while the Airbus A320 and Boeing's 737-800 were evaluated as replacement for Boeing's 757-258s. After two years of evaluation, Boeing's New Generation 737s were selected and an order for two Boeing 737-700 series and three Boeing 737-800 series was placed. They were delivered in 1999.

Boeing 737-758s are each equipped with a pair of CFM International CFM56-7B24 turbofan engines with 24,200lbf (108kN) of maximum thrust. Each could carry 110 passengers in a two-class cabin seating arrangement (16 business class seats and 94 economy class seats). The aircraft with c/n 29960/327 and 29961/442 flew for the first time at Everett Airport, Boeing's Paine Field facility, on 8 July and 29 November 1999, respectively. They received r/c 4X-EKD and 4X-EKE under the AOC of El Al before their deliveries took place on 11 August and 14 December 1999, respectively. In Israel, they also received fleet numbers and the names 804 *Ashkelon* and 702 *Nazareth*.

The three Boeing 737-858s, which El Al received in 1999 had c/n 29957/204, 29958/249 and 29959/314. Their deliveries took place on 24 February, 21 April and 31 July 1999, respectively. They received r/c 4X-EKA, 4X-EKB and 4X-EKC and fleet numbers 801–803 and names *Tiberias*, *Eilat* and *Beit Shean*.

The 737-800 seats 162 to 189 passengers, depending on the configuration. El Al chose to configure them with 146 seats in two classes initially, however, this was later changed. Today r/c 4X-EKR, which is in use by Sun D'Or, has full economy seats for 189 passengers while the rest of the fleet has a two-class seating configuration.

With the deliveries of the Boeing 737-758s, El Al retired its two Boeing 737-258s and sold them to Nationwide Airlines in South Africa, in April 2000. Following the deliveries of the Boeing 737-858s, two Boeing 757-258s were phased out. They were 4X-EBR and 4X-EBI, which had been operated by the airline since 19 July 1988 and 24 March 1997. The first aircraft was owned by the airline while the second had been leased from ILFC. El Al subleased its Boeing 737-258s to Arkia for several years and then Israel's Aeroel Airways during the last year of service.

On 26 March 2002, El Al added a fourth B738 to its fleet but this time under a long-term leasing contract. It was a three-year old Boeing 737-86N owned by GECAS with c/n 28587/192, which had been delivered in February 1999. The aircraft with r/c N802NA was leased to North American Airlines before being leased to El Al on 26 March 2002. It was operated by the airline with r/c 4X-EKI and fleet name *Modi'in-Maccabim-Re'ut*.

Two more B738s were added to the fleet in 2005 and 2006. They were a Boeing 737-86Q with c/n 30287/1308, built in 2003, and owned by Aviation Capital Group, and a Boeing 737-8Q8 with c/n 30639/935, built in 2001, and owned by ILFC and then Carlyle Aviation Partners. They received r/c 4X-EKO and 4X-EKP and were put into use by the airline from October 2005 and January 2006, respectively, under long-term leasing contracts. They received fleet names *Lod* and *Nahariya*.

On 25 August and 31 December 2008, El Al received two Boeing 747-8HXs with c/n 36433/2702 and 29638/2766 that had first flown on 5 August 2008 and 16 December 2008. Both are owned by Aviation Capital Group (ACG), an aircraft leasing company, and have been operated under long-term leasing contracts. They received r/c 4X-EKS and 4X-EKF and fleet names *Caesarea* and *Kinneret*.

Boeing 738s

Three more aircraft were added to the fleet in 2009, which were procured by the airline instead of being leased. They were all Boeing 737-85Ps with c/n 35485/2871, 35486/2908 and 35487/2819 that had been built for Air Europa but as that airline cancelled, El Al purchased them all. They were delivered to El Al with r/c 4X-EKH, 4X-EKJ and 4X-EKL on 18 April, 21 May and 22 June 2009 and received fleet names *Yarden*, *Degania* and *Nahalal*. With their deliveries, the number of B738s operated by the airline increased to 11 of which six were owned by El Al.

Between 2010 and 2020, five more B738s were added to El Al's fleet, all with long-term leasing contracts. They were 4X-EKT (c/n 33030/1968) owned by CIT Aerospace from November 2010; 4X-EKM (c/n 30465/502) owned by Babcock and Brown Aircraft Management (BBAM) from 11 May 2012; 4X-EKR (c/n 30466/505) owned by BBAM from 16 May 2012; 4X-EKU (c/n 33834/1938) owned by Macquarie Air Finance from March 2013; and 4X-EKK (c/n 39070/5196) owned by BBAM from 14 February 2020. They received fleet names *Bet Shemesh*, *Fall*, *Givatayim*, *London* and *Giv'at Shmuel*.

In 2023, El Al also added a Cargo Boeing 737-86N to its fleet. The aircraft, owned by Genesis Aircraft Services, had c/n 33004 and had been built in 2002. It was converted into a cargo aircraft in Guangzhou Baiyun International Airport, in June 2023. The aircraft has r/c 4X-EKZ with El Al.

When this book was written in October 2023, El Al had 14 airworthy B738s, with r/c 4X-EKB, 4X-EKC, 4X-EKF, 4X-EKH, 4X-EKI, 4X-EKJ, 4X-EKK, 4X-EKL, 4X-EKM, 4X-EKO, 4X-EKP, 4X-EKS, 4X-EKT and 4X-EKU. One more aircraft, with r/c 4X-EKA, was stored at Ben Gurion Airport. Another, with r/c 4X-EKK, was returned to its lessor, while 4X-EKR was transferred to El Al's subsidiary, Sun D'Or.

For five years, between November 2013 and October 2018, Up, the low-cost airline brand owned by El Al, operated four B738s with r/c 4X-EKO, 4X-EKM, 4X-EKT and 4X-EKU. They received a distinctive colour scheme of a blue cloudy sky on their fuselage while their vertical stabiliser livery remained unchanged. They connected Tel Aviv to Larnaca, Prague, Berlin, Budapest and Kyiv. The last Up flight was on 14 October 2018, after which it ceased trading.

Future Fleet

In August 2023, El Al's B738s flew to 33 destinations: Amsterdam, Athens, Barcelona, Batumi, Berlin, Bucharest, Budapest, Casablanca, Dubai, Dublin, Frankfurt, Geneva, Istanbul, Larnaca, Lisbon, London, Paris, Paphos, Madrid, Marseille, Marrakesh, Milan, Munich, Nice, Venice, Vienna, Rome, Rhodes, Sofia, Sharm el-Sheikh, Tbilisi, Thessaloniki and Zürich.

As of August 2023, all of El Al's B739ERs were airworthy and flying to 27 destinations including Amsterdam, Athens, Barcelona, Berlin, Budapest, Dublin, Dubai, Frankfurt, Geneva, Istanbul, Larnaca, Lisbon, London, Madrid, Marseille, Marrakesh, Milan, Moscow, Munich, Nice, Paris, Rome, Rhodes, Sofia, Venice, Vienna and Zürich.

4X-EKD and 4X-EKE, El Al's two Boeing 737-758s were sold to Capstar Aviation LLC in Austin, Texas, in 2016. Six years later, in 2022, El Al began reviewing the Airbus A321neo and Boeing 737 MAX as potential replacements for its Boeing Next Generation 737-800 and 900 aircraft, which are likely to retire in the mid-2030s. On 10 August 2023, El Al's CEO, Dina Ben Tal Ganancia informed Reuters that there would be a possible deal for as many as 30 A321neo aircraft allowing the retirement of the B738s by 2030 and B739ERs by 2032.

El Al with a fleet of one cargo aircraft and 43 passenger aircraft, including 23 Boeing Next Generation 737s, intends to increase the number of its aircraft to 59 in 2028 enabling it to achieve a US$3.5bn annual revenue and carry 7.7 million passengers in that year. To reach this goal, El Al will need at least 16 more passenger aircraft.

Boeing 737-758 with r/c 4X-EKD is at Zürich Airport on 28 January 2006. (Gavin GH@BHD)

4X-EKE, the second Boeing 737-758 operated by El Al is in Zürich on 9 February 2005. (Aero Icarus)

4X-EKA, El Al's first Boeing 737-858 during its unveiling ceremony at Ben Gurion Airport. 4X-EKA was in storage in October 2023. (Moshe Milner/Israel Government Press Office)

Delivered on 21 April 1999, 4X-EKB was one of the three Boeing 737-858s built specially for El Al. It is in Zürich on 13 April 2013. (Keld Bonfizz)

4X-EKC, an El Al Boeing 737-858 is at Zürich on 15 January 2010. (Aero Icarus)

This Boeing 737-85P was built by Boeing for Air Europa in 2009 but was not taken by the company and was instead delivered to El Al on 21 May 2009. The aircraft is in Zürich on 16 January 2017. (Gavin GH@BHD)

4X-EKL is a Boeing 737-85P ordered by Air Europa but delivered to El Al as a part of its orders on 22 June 2009. (Gavin GH@BHD)

4X-EKS, a Boeing 737-8HX in use by El Al under a long-term leasing contract with Aviation Capital Group aircraft leasing company, on 23 January 2019. (Gavin GH@BHD)

This Boeing 737-85P with r/c 4X-EKH is taking off from Zürich Airport on 26 November 2016. (Aero Icarus)

4X-EKU, an El Al Boeing 737-8Z9 in the colours of its subsidiary airline, Up, at Larnaca, Cyprus, on 23 October 2017. (Babak Taghvaee)

After El Al disbanded its subsidiary airline Up, the Boeing 737s that were in its use, including 4X-EKU, were rebranded with the El Al name but kept Up's livery. It is at Larnaca, Cyprus, on 12 September 2018. (Babak Taghvaee)

4X-EKU in El Al's colours. It is at Charles de Gaulle Airport on 15 August 2023. (Babak Taghvaee)

This El Al Boeing 737-86N with r/c 4X-EKN was operated by North American Airlines between 1999 and 2002 before being leased to El Al from 26 March 2002. Sun D'Or International operated it between 2015 and 2019. It is at Charles de Gaulle Airport on 22 August 2023. (Babak Taghvaee)

Up operated this Boeing 737-86Q with r/c 4X-EKO between 2014 and 2018. After its return to El Al, it remained branded with Up's livery for a number of years. It is at Athens on 22 August 2018. (Babak Taghvaee)

El Al has leased this Boeing 737-804 from Babcock and Brown Aircraft Management since 2012. Up operated it between 2014 and 2018. After the disbandment of Up, El Al operated it in Up's colours until it was returned to the standard colours of the airline. It is in Athens in August 2018. (Babak Taghvaee)

4X-EKR is a Boeing 737-804 that has been leased from Babcock and Brown Aircraft Management under a long-term contract since 2012. Since 2015, Sun D'Or has operated it, performing charter flights to tourist destinations such as Larnaca, where it was photographed on 15 May 2023. (Babak Taghvaee)

Boeing 737-958ER: 2013–Today

El Al retired 4X-EBS, one of its three last remaining Boeing 757-258s from service in April 2009 and the remaining two examples, r/c 4X-EBU and 4X-EBV, on 27 and 6 November 2012, respectively. Eight Boeing 737-958ERs, which El Al received between 2013 and 2017, were later operated to carry passengers on routes previously covered by the Boeing 757s. The aircraft are 4X-EHA (c/n 41552/4632), 4X-EHB (c/n 41553/4697), 4X-EHC (c/n 41554/4990), 4X-EHD (c/n 41555/5311), 4X-EHE (c/n 41556/4840), 4X-EHF (c/n 41557/5775), 4X-EHH (c/n 41558/5791) and 4X-EHI (c/n 41559/5818). They were named *Kiryat Ono, Kiryat Bialik, Kiryat Ata, Kiryat Gat, Kiryat Tiv'on, Kiryat Yam, Kiryat Motzkin* and *Kiryat Malakhi*.

The design and development of the Boeing 737-900 began in 1997 as a stretched variant of the B738, capable of carrying 180 to 215 passengers. The prototype first flew on 3 August 2000. It retained the maximum take-off weight (MTOW), fuel capacity, trading range for payload and door configurations of the -800 series. Later, the Boeing 737-900ER (Extended Range) was developed with an additional pair of exit doors and a flat rear pressure bulkhead enabling an increase in seating capacity to 180 (for two classes) and 220 (if arranged as economy class only). It was built as a replacement for the Boeing 757-200s and as a competitor to Airbus A321.

In 2013, El Al received its first two Boeing 737-958ERs – 4X-EHA and 4X-EHB, with their deliveries taking place on 9 October and 27 November 2013, respectively. El Al received six B739ERs: 4X-EHC, 4X-EHD, 4X-EHE, 4X-EHF, 4X-EHH and 4X-EHI on 9 July 2014, 11 March 2015, 26 March 2014, 14 February 2016, 27 February 2017 and 16 March 2016, respectively. They had a pair of CFM56-7B27E turbofan engines, which were more powerful than the CFM56-7B24 and CFM56-7B26s of the Boeing 737-700 and -800 series.

4X-EHA featured the new Boeing Sky Interior. This interior is the latest in a series of enhancements for both airlines and passengers. It introduces new LED lighting and curved architecture that welcomes passengers on board and creates a greater sense of spaciousness and comfort in the cabin. The interior also features modern, sculpted sidewalls and overhead bins that disappear into the ceiling, and had roomier capacity. The aircraft was equipped with a two-class seating cabin configuration for 16 business class seats and 159 economy class seats.

Compared to Boeing 737-858s, these Boeing 737-958ERs are younger and are expected to remain in service for at least five more years after the retirement of their shorter cousins. At the time of writing in October 2023, the aircraft were all airworthy and were charted by the Israeli Defence Forces for repatriation of thousands of active and reservist troops from across Europe to Tel Aviv between 8 and 18 October 2023 in order to take part in Operation *Iron Swords* against Hamas. The operation was launched on October 7 in response to a terror attack by Hamas in which 1,350 Israelis and other nationals were killed in the villages around the Gaza Strip and 199 Israeli and other nationals were kidnapped.

The Self-Protection Systems of El Al's Boeing 737s

On 28 November 2002, 4X-BAW, a Boeing 757-3E7 of Arkia carrying 271 passengers and crew was attacked. Two 9K32 Strela-2 shoulder-fired, surface-to-air missiles were fired at the aircraft and missed it. The incident happened after its departure from Mombasa-Moi International Airport in Kenya and led

4X-EHA, El Al's first Boeing 737-958ER is at Frankfurt on 22 July 2016. (Keld Bonfizz)

to the design and development of self-protection systems for Israeli passenger aircraft from the threats of surface-to-air and air-to-air missiles.

During wartime, when the threat of MANPADS (Man-Portable Air-Defence Systems) being used by Palestinian terrorist groups against Israeli passenger aircraft increases, El Al has a Directed Infra-Red Countermeasure (DIRCM) self-protection system named C-MUSIC installed on its Boeing 737s, which was designed, developed and built by Elbit Systems. Prior to take-off or landing, pilots activate the system and its infra-red sensor searches for heat-seeking missiles. If a missile is detected, the system dispenses flares to warn about the incoming missile or missiles so that pilots can take precautionary manoeuvres, such as a rapid banking to reduce the chance of a missile hitting the aircraft.

C-MUSIC is an integrated electronic warfare (EW) suite in a single line replaceable unit (LRU), with comprehensive, advanced Electronic Warfare (EW) capabilities. It comprises an EWC (Electronic Warfare Controller), digital RWR (Radar Warning Receiver), PAWS (IR Missile Warning System), LWS (Laser Warning System) and CFD (Chaff/Flare Dispensing) system. It took less than one week for Elbit Systems to modify each aircraft to carry the C-MUSIC pod beneath the empennage and to carry out the necessary wiring and installation of a control panel for the system on the aircraft's instrument panel. 4X-EKA, El Al's Boeing 738 was the first to be fitted with the system and flew with the system operational in June 2013 after successful completion of tests. Today, all El Al Boeing 737-858/958ERs and Boeing 777-228ERs can be equipped during wartime with self-protection systems.

El Al Airlines: Israel's National Airline

4X-EHD, El Al's fourth Boeing 737-958ER, is departing Athens International Airport on 9 June 2022; its self-protection system is installed under its empennage. (Babak Taghvaee)

Boeing 737-958ER with r/c 4X-EHE is landing in Frankfurt on 31 March 2017. (Keld Bonfizz)

The Narrow-Body Jetliners

4X-EHH is in Athens on 27 April 2023. (Babak Taghvaee)

4X-EHH, an El Al Boeing 737-958ERs, departs Ben Gurion Airport on 12 February 2023. (Hezi Shmueli)

Chapter 3
The Wide-Body Jetliners

Boeing 747-258B/C/F: 1971–2011

In 1968, one year before the first flight of the Boeing 747, the first wide-body passenger aircraft designed and manufactured in the US, El Al became one of its first customers. The prototype Boeing 747 logged its first flight on 9 February 1969, four years after the launch of the design and development of the aircraft. Two years later, El Al received its first examples: two Boeing 747-258Bs with r/c 4X-AXA and 4X-AXB.

The design and development of what became the Boeing 747 began with Boeing Commercial Airplanes in the early 1990s. It initially had a military use to meet the needs of the United States Air Force (USAF) to provide a heavy transport aircraft. However, it lost out to Lockheed's C-5A Galaxy, and later turned into a successful product in the wide-body passenger aircraft market. El Al closely monitored the development of the Boeing 747 and saw it as a suitable aircraft to carry 350–400 passengers between Tel Aviv and New York.

As the Boeing 747-100 series lacked powerful enough engines to meet the needs of El Al, the airline selected the -200B series equipped with four Pratt & Whitney JT9D-7 turbofan engines, capable of producing 20,250kg (45,000lb) thrust each compared to the JT9D-3s of the -100 series. On 25 January 1968, El Al ordered two Boeing 747s which were later manufactured as 200B series with c/n 20135 and 20274. They rolled out of the factory on 28 April and 16 September 1971, and received r/c 4X-AXA and 4X-AXB. They were delivered on 26 May and 22 November 1971, respectively.

The two Boeing 747s were painted in a new scheme designed by Israeli artist Dan Reisinger. The paint scheme later became the standard livery for all El Al's aircraft and was used for 30 years. The aircraft's cabin interior was also designed by El Al with light colours creating a bright atmosphere for passengers. While the upper floor was dedicated to business class passengers, the lower floor was for economy class passengers.

The first Boeing 747 with r/c 4X-AXA was delivered during a ceremony at Everett, Washington, attended by El Al's Boeing 747 pilots and flight engineer, Mordechai Ben-Ari, CEO of El Al at that time, and Leah Rabin, the wife of the Israel's Ambassador to the US. The aircraft was flown to Tel Aviv on 2 June 1971. The aircraft was unveiled the next day during a ceremony attended by Prime Minister Golda Meir, Transport Minister Shimon Peres, El Al Chairman Moshe Carmel and President Mordechai Ben-Ari. Six days later, the aircraft entered commercial use and had its first flight from Tel Aviv to New York with a stopover in London on 8 June 1971. The second aircraft, which was delivered on 22 November 1971, was also used for transatlantic flights with a stopover in Paris.

The Boeing 747s allowed El Al to carry almost three times more passengers and cargo to John F. Kennedy International Airport, New York, than its Boeing 707-358/458s. El Al acquired a third Boeing 747-258B in 1971. The aircraft with c/n 20704 and test r/c N1799B logged its first flight on 5 April 1973. The aircraft was the first Boeing 747-200B to be equipped with more powerful JT9D-7AW turbofans that increased the maximum take-off weight of the aircraft to 356,070kg (785,000lb).

The third Boeing 747-258B was delivered on 18 April 1973 and received r/c 4X-AXC. Its introduction enabled El Al to offer non-stop flights from Tel Aviv to New York from 29 April 1973. For a direct flight, usually 380 passengers were carried with no cargo on board. With the introduction of more powerful

Pratt & Whitney JT9D-7F engines, the Boeing 747-258Cs could carry a full complement of passengers as well as heavy cargo.

In 1978, El Al ordered its fourth Boeing 747-258B; c/n 22254 first flew on 6 December 1979. It was delivered to El Al on 21 December 1979 and received r/c 4X-AXH in its service. In August 1992, the aircraft was sent to the Boeing factory to be equipped with a side cargo door (SCD) and be converted to special freighter (SF). After modification and conversion work, it was redelivered on 14 January 1993. At that time, El Al had five other Boeing 747s capable of carrying large cargo; two were combi, while three others were pure freighters.

Combi and Cargo Jumbo Jets

El Al's Boeing 747-258Bs could carry 13,500kg (29,769lb) of cargo in addition to passengers. The maximum cargo volume and weight loaded into the cargo compartment of Boeing 747-258B passenger aircraft was less than the amount of the cargo carried by the Boeing 707-358C cargo aircraft of the airline, therefore El Al acquired a Boeing 747-200C in December 1975. The -200C was a combi or convertible passenger/cargo aircraft equipped with a side cargo door, similar to those of the Boeing 707-358Cs, enabling loading and unloading of large cargo. The Boeing 747-258C with c/n 21190 was delivered to El Al on 31 December 1975. It received r/c 4X-AXD on 11 April 1976.

Due to the increased demand for air cargo, El Al acquired a secondhand Boeing 747-124F aircraft, which was a cargo aircraft. The aircraft had been built as a passenger aircraft following an order from Continental Airlines. It was acquired by the Imperial Iranian Air Force (IIAF) alongside 11 other Boeing 747s in 1975. It was converted to freighter (-124F) for the IIAF. After just two years of service in Iran with s/n 5-291 and 5-8112, it was later sold to Boeing. El Al acquired it on 21 June 1977 and operated it with r/c 4X-AXZ.

El Al ordered a second Boeing 747-258C, which was manufactured with c/n 21594 and was first flown on 7 June 1978. It was delivered to El Al on 16 June 1978 and received r/c 4X-AXF on 17 June 1978. Next, El Al procured another pure cargo aircraft, this time from Boeing Commercial. The aircraft with c/n 21737 was first flown on 7 March 1979. It was delivered to El Al on 19 March 1979 and received r/c 4X-AXG in its service.

From Expansion of the Boeing 747 Fleet to Retirement

Despite procurement of Boeing 767-258ER wide-body passenger aircraft and their use for transatlantic flights, El Al continued operating its Boeing 747-258B/C/Fs as well as its sole Boeing 747-124F but also acquired more second-hand classic Boeing 747s between 1989 and 2004. They were two Boeing 747-245Fs with c/n 22150 and 22151, both built in 1980 and previously operated by Flying Tiger Line, Federal Express and Singapore Airlines. They were acquired by El Al in 1995 and 1992, respectively, and they were operated with r/c 4X-AXL and 4X-AXK by the airline.

In addition to the Boeing 747-245Fs, El Al acquired an ex-Korean Air Boeing 747-2B5B(F) with c/n 22485, which was built in 1981 and had been operated by Korean Air until 1992, when it was retired and was later converted to freighter by Boeing. An Israeli airline named Cargo Air Lines acquired and operated it with r/c 4X-ACN from 26 June 2003 until 10 December 2004 when it was sold to El Al and received r/c 4X-AXM.

In addition, a second-hand Boeing 747-200B series aircraft was also acquired. The Boeing 747-238B with 20841 had been manufactured for Qantas in 1974. After 14 years of service, it was retired and sold to El Al and received r/c 4X-AXQ on 7 May 1988. It was delivered to the airline on 8 May 1988 and leased to its previous owner, Quantas, from 5 September 1988 to 23 May 1989.

On 4 October 1992, El Al lost one of its Boeing 747-258Fs in Amsterdam. The aircraft with r/c 4X-AXG crashed after two of its engines got separated from the aircraft's wing after their pylons broke. The aircraft crashed into an apartment complex resulting in the death of the crew and 39 people on the ground. After determining the cause of the accident, El Al had its Boeing 747 engine pylons modified by IAI's facility.

El Al retired its remaining 11 classic Boeing 747s between 1999 and 2011. They were 4X-AXA (retired in October 1999), 4X-AXB (retired in November 2001), 4X-AXC (retired on 28 October 2001), 4X-AXD (retired on 29 October 2000), 4X-AXF (retired in August 2008), 4X-AXH (retired on 12 July 2006), 4X-AXK (retired in February 2010), 4X-AXL (retired on 11 November 2011), 4X-AXM (retired in 2008), 4X-AXQ (retired in 2005) and 4X-AXZ (retired in March 1999).

The sole Boeing 747-124F was leased to AVIANCA in Colombia and received Colombian r/c HK-2400 on 21 July 1981. It was returned to El Al and received r/c 4X-AXZ again in July 1982. It became a famous aircraft among the fleet as it was operated with its distinctive AVIANCA red livery until repainted in El Al colours during its D check. The two Boeing 747-258Cs with r/c 4X-AXD and 4X-AXF were also leased to Cargo Air Lines in the final years of their service with the airline.

Most of El Al's Boeing 747-100/200 aircraft remained unsold and stored in Tel Aviv until they were scrapped. Only 4X-AXC and 4X-AXH were sold. 4X-AXC was sold to the Israel Airports Authority for fire-fighting practice. It was destroyed during a fire practice at Tel Aviv on 30 June 2008. 4X-AXH was sold to Thesis Airlines and was operated from October 2006 until 17 October 2008. It was scrapped in July 2014.

The only Boeing 747 that survived for several years after its retirement was 4X-AXM. It was stored in Tel Aviv and used for fire practice with Ben Gurion Airport fire department. The aircraft, which still had its distinctive Korean Air paint, was scrapped in 2022.

In addition to the 12 classic Boeing 747-100/200 series aircraft owned by El Al, the airline also operated eight other classic Boeing 747s under short-term dry- and wet-leasing contracts for both cargo and passenger transport. Among them c/n 24106 was a Boeing 747-341 with r/c TF-ATH belonging to Air Atlanta Iceland. The other aircraft were a Boeing 747-273C of World Airways with r/c N748WA, three Boeing 747-123(SF)s of Flying Tiger Line (N801FT, N803FT and N804FT), a Boeing 747-131 of GATX Leasing with r/c N93117, a Boeing 747-271C of Cargolux with r/c LX-BCV and a Boeing 747-228F of the same airline with r/c 4X-DCV.

El Al's Jumbo Jets During Evacuation Operations

El Al's Boeing 747-258B/C/Fs and its sole Boeing 747-124F have participated in several notable evacuation operations to save lives. In February 1979, Iran's secular government of Pahlavi was overthrown by Islamists and Marxists. After the fall of the Shah's government, an Islamic totalitarian state was formed, spearheaded by Ruhollah Khomeini, leader of the Islamic Revolution. The Islamists who opposed the Shah received support from the PFLP and other countries such as Libya and Syria. From this point, Iran terminated its close relationship with Israel.

Islamist and Marxist terrorist groups carried out attacks against foreign nationals in Iran during the last months of the Kingdom of Mohammad-Reza Shah Pahlavi. Israeli nationals including the 32 employees of El Al based in Tehran became a target.

Before the Islamic Revolution, several Israeli construction companies operated in Iran including at air bases of the Imperial Iranian Air Force. El Al's Boeing 747-258C/Fs were used to airlift construction equipment from Israel to Iran. The same aircraft were used to supply tons of fruit and vegetables, eggs and chicken to Iran on a weekly basis. The Boeing 747-258Bs, 707-358B/Cs, 707-458Bs also flew passengers between Tehran and Tel Aviv on a weekly basis as more than 150,000 Iranian nationals lived in Israel at that time.

The Shah left Iran on 16 January 1979 but before that, it was clear that his government was falling apart. On 24 December 1978, Islamists began protesting against Israel in front of El Al's building in

Tehran, and a few days later, they attacked the building. From December 1978, thousands of Iranian Jews, Muslims and Christians fleeing Iran bought tickets from El Al increasing the airline's flights to Tehran despite strikes at Mehrabad International Airport.

Aviation fuel was unavailable in Tehran, so Boeing 747s were mostly used for the evacuation flights. El Al's flights to Iran finally stopped on 10 February 1979, several days after the arrival of Ruhollah Khomeini from Paris. In August 1980, El Al's building was burned down by Mojahedin Khalq Organisation (MKO), a terrorist group with close ties to PFLP. The building was later confiscated by Khomeini's foundation.

In May 1991, El Al's Boeing 747s were used to evacuate thousands of Ethiopian Jews from Addis Ababa. The evacuation flights took place as part of Operation *Solomon*, which was carried out in just three days following an agreement between the Israeli and Ethiopian governments and rebel forces. The Israeli government paid US$35m to the Ethiopian government, which enabled the evacuation of 14,000 out of the 20,000 Ethiopian Jews.

Under command of Amnon Lipkin-Shahak, then deputy chief of staff of the Israeli Defence Forces, the operation was launched on 24 May 1991 during which Boeing 747-258Cs had their galleys removed to make space for 760 passenger seats for the flight. 4X-AXF was to fly to Addis Ababa on 24 May. To maximise the number of passengers flown, each person could carry a small bag and some clothes. Boeing 747s operated 11 flights to transport 7,000 people.

During one of these flights, 4X-AXF airlifted 1,122 passengers across the 2,575km (1,600-mile) long journey, which lasted three hours and 15 minutes. The remaining Ethiopian Jews were evacuated using at least six C-130E/H Hercules medium transport aircraft, one Boeing KC-707 Israeli Air Force tanker aircraft, and one Ethiopian Airlines Boeing 757. El Al also involved its other aircraft types in the operation. They were a Boeing 767-258ET with r/c 4X-EAB which carried 430 people, and a Boeing 757-258 with r/c 4X-EBR carrying 360 people.

All three Boeing 747-258Bs with r/c 4X-AXA, 4X-AXB and 4X-AXC at Ben Gurion Airport during a strike on 1 October 1975. (Moshe Milner/Israel Government Press Office)

4X-AXB, the second Boeing 747-258B at Ben Gurion Airport on 1 October 1975. (Moshe Milner/Israel Government Press Office)

A multinational force of UN soldiers disembark, on 17 March 1982, from El Al's first Boeing 747-258B with r/c 4X-AXA in Sharm el-Sheikh to guard the Sinai and be a buffer force between Israel and Egypt, during the implementation of the peace agreements between the countries. (Sa'ar Ya'akov/Israel Government Press Office)

4X-AXD, a Boeing 747-258Cs is at Munich on 15 October 1978. (Stefan Röhrich/Munich-Riem Aviation Photos)

4X-AXF, the second Boeing 747-258C is in Munich in February 1979. (Norbert Kröpfl/Munich-Riem Aviation Photos)

4X-AXH, a Boeing 747-258BM, was operated by El Al between 21 December 1979 and 17 October 2008. It is at Tel Aviv-Ben Gurion Airport on 22 April 1999. (Sa'ar Ya'acov/Israel Government Press Office)

This ex-Singaporean Airlines Boeing 747-245F was operated by El Al between 1995 and 2011. It is landing at Heathrow Airport in the early 2000s. (Ramb Dub)

4X-AXZ, a Boeing 747-124(SF), was operated by El Al between 1977 and 1999. It is at Ben Gurion Airport in September 1977. (Moshe Milner/Israel Government Press Office)

Between July 1981 and July 1982, El Al leased this Boeing 747-124(SF) to Avianca and as a result, it was painted in the colours of that company. After its return to El Al Cargo, the aircraft kept this distinctive paint scheme for a number of years. It is in Paris in June 1983. (Keld Bonfizz)

On the right, President Ezer Weizmann in the cockpit of a Boeing 747, on his way to state visits in Europe on 5 May 1995. The aircraft appears to be 4X-AXA, the first El Al Boeing 747-258B. (Ya'acov Sa'ar/Israel Government Press Office)

El Al chartered this Boeing 747-123(SF) with r/c N801FT from Flying Tiger Line between 21 August 1977 and 1 July 1978. (Norbert Kröpfl/Munich-Riem Aviation Photos)

This ex-Korean Air's Boeing 747-2B5BF SCD was operated by El Al with r/c 4X-AXM between 2004 and 2009. It is in Amsterdam on 30 July 2008. (Ramb Dub)

Boeing 747-412/458: 1994–2019

Boeing designed and developed an improved model of the Boeing 747 named the -400 series and nicknamed the super jumbo jet. Compared to the -300 series, it had the extended upper level of fuselage but was equipped with modern avionic systems with a glass cockpit. With its sophisticated computers, the aircraft no longer required flight engineers, thus its flight crew was reduced from three to two. The -400 series had 1.8m (6ft) wingtip extensions and winglets of the same height enabling improvements in fuel efficiency and economy of four per cent compared to the classic jumbo jets.

In addition to the wing refinements, Boeing also fitted the -400 series with tail fuel tanks, which alongside the improved fuel economy due to winglets, increased the range of the aircraft. The new generation of turbofan engines has a lower fuel burn compared to the those of the classic and this too, helped increase the range. Boeing 747-400 series were marketed with different types of engines: Pratt & Whitney PW4062, General Electric CF6-80C2, and Rolls-Royce RB211-524.

Boeing made the Model 747-400 series in passenger (-400), freighter (-400F), combi (-400M), domestic (-400D), extended range passenger (-400ER), and extended range freighter (-400ERF) versions. The -400 passenger variants had the same upper deck as the -300 series while the cargo or freighter variants had short upper decks similar to -100 to -200 series. A less popular version of the aircraft, named 747-400D, was also developed and built for short-range operations with a maximum seating for 624 passengers, while also having wingtips. Boeing manufactured 694 Boeing 747-400 series aircraft including four Boeing 747-458s for El Al.

In 1993, El Al procured its first two Boeing 747-400 series aircraft while the third was procured in 1994. These three aircraft became the flagship El Al aircraft taking over most of the flights, including transatlantic ones. El Al ordered its -400 aircraft with Pratt & Whitney PW4000 engines that had 14 per cent less fuel burn and significantly fewer noise emissions when compared with the JT9D turbofans. With these engines and the structural and aerodynamic design refinements, the aircraft had an increased maximum take-off weight of 425 tonnes (32 tonnes more than -200 series). These powerful engines also enabled an increased cruise speed which reduced the journey time between New York and Tel Aviv by 30 minutes.

El Al's Boeing Model 747-400 series aircraft were named Boeing 747-458. C/n 26055, 26056 and 27915 logged their first flights on 11 April 1994, 18 May 1994 and 15 May 1995, respectively. They received r/c 4X-ELA, 4X-ELB and 4X-ELC, fleet numbers 201–203 and fleet names *Tel Aviv-Jaffa*, *Haifa* and *Be'er Sheva*. They were delivered to El Al on 27 April, 27 May 1994 and 31 May 1995. In 1998, El Al acquired a fourth Boeing 747-458; c/n 29328 was delivered on 24 May 1999. It received r/c 4X-ELD, fleet number 204 and was named *Jerusalem*.

Between 2005 and 2010, El Al acquired four ex-Singapore Airlines' Boeing 747-400 series. Three were Boeing 747-412 passenger carriers with c/n 26551, 26555 and 27132 while the last was a Boeing 747-412F freighter or cargo carrier with c/n 26563. The Boeing 747-412s received r/c 4X-ELE, 4X-ELH and 4X-ELS with their deliveries taking place on 28 October 2008, February 2011 and 18 February 2005, respectively. In service with El Al, 4X-ELE and 4X-ELH received fleet numbers 205 and 208 and were named *Rishon LeTsiyon* and *Ashdod*, while 4X-ELS was withdrawn from use and never received a fleet name or number.

Among these ex-Singaporean Airlines' Boeing 747-412/412Fs, r/c 4X-ELH was operated by El Al under a long-term leasing contract. The Boeing 747-412F delivered in April 2010 with r/c 4X-ELF, fleet number 207 and named *Hoopoe*, operated under a similar long-term leasing contract. The lessor 4X-ELF was Bank of America Leasing (Ireland) Company and the lessor of 4X-ELH was R. B. Leasing.

El Al's Boeing 747-400 series passenger and cargo aircraft were withdrawn from service by the end of 2019. R/c 4X-ELS, a Boeing 747-412 previously operated by Singapore Airlines was retired shortly after its procurement on 27 September 2006 and was later sold to Cathay Pacific Airways on 14 March 2007. The 1994-built 4X-ELE, another Boeing 747-412, retired next after its final flight on 28 December 2017.

4X-ELA, the first Boeing 747-458 is landing at Ben Gurion Airport on 3 May 2005. (Sa'ar Ya'acov/Israel Government Press Office)

It had accumulated a large number of flying hours and cycles and its D check, or overhaul, was seen as non-economic for the airline. It was stored and then scrapped at Ben Gurion Airport with its useful parts being used by the rest of El Al's aircraft.

The remaining six Boeing 747-400 series were all retired in 2019. They were 4X-ELA, 4X-ELB, 4X-ELC, 4X-ELD, 4X-ELF and 4X-ELH, which were retired on 1 November, 1 November, 3 November, 15 September, 1 July and 13 June 2019, respectively. 4X-ELC was the last of them to be retired after its final commercial service from Rome to Tel Aviv on 3 November 2019. 4X-ELD is currently stored in Tel Aviv with almost all of its valuable parts removed; El Al has scrapped all other Boeing 747s.

In addition to these, El Al also operated a Wamos Air Boeing 747-419 under a two-year lease (2016–18). The aircraft, which was built in 1998, was equipped with four General Electric CF6-80C2B1F turbofan engines unlike the El Al Boeing 747-412/458s, which had Pratt & Whitney PW4056 turbofan engines.

In service with El Al, the Boeing 747-458s had three different cabin seating configurations including 47 for first class, 34 for business class and 314 for economy class. The three Boeing 747-412s had three different passenger seating configurations. 4X-ELE had four cabin class seatings for 371 passengers; 12 first class, 50 business class, 39 premium economy and 280 economy. 4X-ELH had seating for 435 passengers: 26 were for first class, 40 for business class and 389 for economy class, while 4X-ELS had seats for 478 passengers in three classes; 12 for first class, 42 for business class and 424 for economy class.

Boeing 747-458 with r/c 4X-ELA is flying at 38,000ft on 28 May 2018. (Steve Jones)

4X-ELD, the fourth El Al Boeing 747-458. (Steve Jones)

4X-ELD, the fourth Boeing 747-458, on 10 July 1999, several months after its delivery to El Al. (Israel Government Press Office)

This ex-Singaporean Airlines Boeing 747-412 with r/c 4X-ELE was operated by El Al between 2008 and 2017. It is just a few months from retirement. (Manuel Negrerie)

4X-ELH was a former Singaporean Airlines Boeing 747-412 operated by El Al between 2011 and 2017. It is seen in June 2016. (Manuel Negrerie)

Boeing 767-258ER: 1983–2013

The Boeing 767 is another wide-body passenger aircraft that entered service with El Al. El Al has operated six different Boeing 757-200ER (Extended Range) and seven Boeing 767-300ER series aircraft, with six on long-term leasing contracts. Design and development of the Boeing 767 had started in the early 1970s when the Boeing 747 wide-body passenger aircraft entered service.

As a twin-engined aircraft, it became a competitor of Airbus A300. Several years of work, design and development were complete by 1980 at a cost of US$3.5–4 billion. The initial prototype first flew on 26 September 1981. The first example of this mass-produced aircraft was delivered to its first customer, United Airlines, on 8 September 1982. The original variant of the aircraft entering mass production was the -200 series.

An extended range version, the Boeing 767-200ER, was designed and developed for its first customer El Al. The aircraft's increased range was due to the additional fuel capacity and higher maximum take-off weight of up to 179,000kg (395,000lb) which compared favourably with the basic variant total of 142,900kg (315,000lb). With increased fuel capacity, it could fly for a maximum 12,200km (6,590nmi /7,580 miles), which was almost twice that of the maximum range of the basic variant at 7,200km (3,900nmi/4,500 miles). The Boeing 767-200ER could carry a maximum 245 economy passengers, the same number as the basic version.

On 18 March 1981, two Boeing 767-200s and two Boeing 767-200ERs valued at US$200m, plus two Boeing 737-200s, were ordered. The Boeing 767s with c/n 22972, 22973, 22974 and 22975 and

Two Boeing 757-258(RT)s and a Boeing 767-258ER with r/c 4X-EAA at Ben Gurion Airport on 4 December 1997. (Ya'acov Sa'ar/Israel Government Press Office)

r/c 4X-EAA, 4X-EAB, 4X-EAC and 4X-EAD were delivered on 12 July 1983, 13 September 1983, 26 March 1984 and 1 June 1984. They received fleet numbers 601–604. These four aircraft rolled out of the factory on 1 June, 26 July 1983, 15 February and 14 March 1984. Deliveries of the four Boeing 767s increased the number of El Al's aircraft to 21 in 1984, which included seven Boeing 707s, two Boeing 737s and eight Boeing 747s.

The acquisition of Boeing 767s was a major step towards modernisation of El Al's fleet. The aircraft were equipped with modern avionic systems including electronic instrumentation such as cathode ray tube (CRT) instrument panels. Computers enabled the flight engineer position in the flight deck to be removed reducing the crew to the pilot and co-pilot. El Al's Boeing 767-258s were equipped with powerful Pratt & Whitney JT9D-7R4D turbofan engines, so the aircraft could be operated with the maximum take-off weight. The airline subsequently used pallets instead of cargo containers for carrying luggage and cargo in the lower-deck cargo area. This increased the capacity from 8,900–14,850kg (9.9–16.5 tons) without causing any need to reduce the passenger load.

While the first Boeing 767s were mostly used for European flights, the Boeing 767-258ERs with r/c 4X-EAC and 4X-EAD were dedicated to transatlantic flights. 4X-EAA and 4X-EAB were also later converted to Boeing 767-258ERs.

On 26 March 1984, when the first Boeing 767-258ER was flown to Israel, it made a direct flight from Montreal to Tel Aviv. El Al was the first airline in the world to use a twin-engine wide-body passenger aircraft for a non-stop transatlantic service under the US Federal Aviation Administration (FAA)

regulation for twin-engine wide-body aircraft. Four days after arrival, the first Boeing 767-258ER was used for regular passenger flights to European destinations.

From February 1985, El Al used the Boeing 767-258ERs as replacements for its Boeing 747s for regular flights from Tel Aviv to Los Angeles with occasional stops at Amsterdam and Chicago. They were also used across the Tel Aviv–Amsterdam–Montréal and Tel Aviv–Amsterdam–New York–Miami routes.

On 12 February and 2 April 1999, El Al procured two secondhand Boeing 767-27E(ER) aircraft with c/n 24832 and 24854, both built in 1990. They had been operated by Aéromaritime (Air France subsidiary) from 26 July and 26 September 1990, with r/c F-GHGD and F-GHGE. With El Al, they received r/c 4X-EAE and 4X-EAF, fleet numbers 610 and 611 and fleet names *Mishmar Ha'emek* and *Daliat El Carmel*.

Boeing 767-258ERs with r/c 4X-EAA to 4X-EAD were withdrawn from service on 3 November and 10 August 2008, 27 September and 18 October 2011, while the two Boeing 767-27EERs were retired on 17 May and 13 October 2013, respectively. Among these, just one aircraft with r/c 4X-EAB was sold to AvCorp International, while the others remained unsold. While four of the remaining five were put into storage in Tel Aviv, 4X-EAE was flown to Tupelo Regional Airport, Mississippi, on 23 May 2013, and was scrapped there. After several years of keeping 4X-EAA, 4X-EAC, 4X-EAD and 4X-EAF in storage at Ben Gurion Airport, they too were scrapped between 2011 and 2017. 4X-EAB which had also found a new life in the US was scrapped in 2014.

4X-EAA and 4X-EAB had two-class cabin seating configurations for 198 passengers (24 business class seats and 174 economy class seats) while the rest of the fleet had 191 seats (24 business class and 167 economy class).

4X-EAA, the first El Al Boeing 767-258ER is landing at Heathrow Airport on 10 January 2017. (Lewis Grant)

4X-EAB, the second El Al Boeing 767-258ER is at Amsterdam-Schiphol Airport on 19 April 2007. (Lewis Grant)

Prime Minister Netanyahu surveys the honour guard as he exits Boeing 767-27E(ER) with r/c 4X-ELE at Bucharest Airport during his official visit to Romania on 6 July 2011. (Moshe Milner/Israel Government Press Office)

Boeing 767-300ER Series: 2004–19

In 1985, Boeing began production of Model 767-300, a stretched variant of the Boeing 767-200. It was 6.43m (21ft) longer, which increased the maximum number of passengers flown by the aircraft to 290. The first serial produced Boeing 767-300 series entered service with Japan Airlines. An extended range version, named Boeing 767-300ER, was designed and manufactured with the first entering service with American Airlines in 1988. The aircraft's increased range was made possible

by carrying a greater quantity of fuel, and facilitated an increased maximum take-off weight of 185,000kg (407,000lb). They had more powerful engines than the standard Boeing 767-300s. Boeing provided three types of engines for them: Pratt & Whitney PW4000, General Electric CF6, or Rolls-Royce RB211.

El Al has operated seven Boeing 767-300ER series aircraft; among them one was dry-leased and one was wet-leased. The first, with c/n 25208 and built in 1991, was a Boeing 767-330(ER), which had been

El Al operated this Boeing 767-330ER under a leasing contract with GECAS from 25 March 2004 until 3 February 2009. The aircraft was withdrawn from use on 24 September 2019 and was broken up in September 2020. It is at Charles de Gaulle airport on 9 July 2011. (Aero Icarus)

operated by Ansett Worldwide Aviation Services, Condor, Air Europe Italy, Air Afrique, Volare Airlines, Sobelair and Dutch Caribbean Airlines before its use in Israel. El Al began operating it under a leasing contract with GECAS Aircraft Leasing Company from 25 March 2004 until 3 February 2019. It received r/c 4X-EAJ, fleet number 635 and was named *Bat Yam*.

In 2006, El Al began operating its second and third Boeing 767-300ER series. One of them was a 15-year-old Boeing 767-3Y0 (ER) with c/n 24953 and the other was an 11-year old Boeing 767-352 (ER) with c/n 26262. The first received r/c 4X-EAP, fleet number 634 and was named *Herzliya*. It was put into service from 16 May. The other aircraft received r/c 4X-EAR, fleet number 633 and fleet name *Kfar Saba*. It entered service from 1 August 2006. 4X-EAP was acquired and operated until 14 September 2018 when it was withdrawn from service and sold to Alta Airlines Holdings in November 2018, while 4X-EAR was operated until 12 October 2018 under a long-term leasing contract with AerCap Aircraft Leasing Company.

The remaining four Boeing 767-300ER series that El Al operated under long-term leasing contracts were a Boeing 767-3Q8 (ER) with r/c 4X-EAK (c/n 27600), a Boeing 767-33A (ER) with r/c 4X-EAL (c/n 27477), a Boeing 767-3Q8 (ER) with r/c 4X-EAM (c/n 28132) and a Boeing 767-3Q8 (ER) with r/c 4X-EAN (c/n 27993). El Al began operating them from June 2010, April 2011, January 2012 and October 2015 until 28 March 2018, 20 January 2019, 1 February 2019 and 23 November 2018,

4X-EAR, a Boeing 767-352ER at Marseille Provence Airport on 26 May 2013. (Stuart Carr)

4X-EAM, a Boeing 767-3Q8ER at Tel Aviv on 17 November 2014. (Stuart Carr)

respectively. Among these, 4X-EAK was the only one to be retired early due to damage to its structure and horizontal stabiliser.

During their service with El Al, 4X-EAJ, 4X-EAN and 4X-EAR had two-class cabin seating configurations for 218 passengers comprising 22 first class seats, 28 business class seats and 168 economy class seats. 4X-EAK and 4X-EAM had 228 seats comprising 22 for first class, 28 for business class and 178 for economy class passengers. The remaining two, with r/c 4X-EAL and 4X-EAP, had passenger seats for 215; 30 were first class, 28 were business class and 157 were economy class.

Boeing 777-258ER: 2001–Today

Today, El Al's six Boeing 777-258(ER)s are the largest wide-body and long-haul passenger aircraft in its service. Despite the fact that only three of them were airworthy at the time of writing in October 2023, they are used to connect Israel to several Asian, American and seasonal European destinations. The Covid-19 pandemic and the ban on international travel impacted the Boeing 777 fleet, and all were stored for months. Some are yet to be taken out of storage: 4X-ECA and 4X-ECC are stored in Ben Gurion Airport. Following the end of travel restrictions, El Al restarted operating its Boeing 777s and re-equipped two with a new cabin configuration.

Initially known as Boeing Model 777-200 IGW (increased gross weight), the Boeing 777-200ER is the second variant of this twin-engined and most successful wide-body passenger aircraft ever built by Boeing Commercial. Compared to the basic Boeing 777-200 variant, the Extended Range has additional fuel capacity and an increased maximum take-off weight enabling transoceanic routes. With a 298-tonne (658,000lb) maximum take-off weight, enabled by a pair of engines producing 93,700lbf (417kN) thrust, it has a 13,084km (7,065nmi/8,130 miles) range. The first customer was British Airways, which received its first aircraft on 6 February 1997. In total, 422 were manufactured for 33 customers until 2019. As of 2018, 338 examples of the -200ER are in airline service.

On 27 October 1999, El Al ordered three Boeing 777-200ERs at a total price of US$350m. As a part of the contract, Boeing agreed to purchase products from Israeli Aviation companies to cover at least 50 per cent of the cost. The contract included US$40m dedicated to enabling El Al and subsequently Israeli Aviation Industries (IAI) to set up an overhaul plant for Boeing 777s at Ben Gurion Airport. Equipped with Rolls-Royce Trent 895 turbofan engines, the three Boeing 777-258ERs with c/n 30831, 30832 and 30833 logged their first flights on 11 January, 9 February and 2 April 2001. They were delivered on 29 January, 21 February and 11 April 2001. They received r/c 4X-ECA to 4X-ECC, 101–103 fleet numbers and *Galilee*, *Netanya* and *Hasharon* fleet names.

Named Boeing 777-258ER, they filled the gap between Boeing 767-258ERs and Boeing 747-458s for long-range flights. The Boeing 777-258ERs had a maximum range of 14,300km (8,850 miles) enabling the airline to fly direct to destinations on the west coast of the US and also to destinations in Asia.

El Al ordered three more Boeing 777-258ERs in 2001/2. These aircraft with c/n 33169, 36083 and 36084 were delivered to El Al on 6 June 2002, 23 July 2007 and 8 August 2007, respectively. They received r/c 4X-ECD to 4X-ECF and 104–106 fleet numbers. They were named *Ramat Gan*, *Sderot* and *Kiryat Shemona*.

At the time of writing, two r/c 4X-ECA and 4X-ECC were in storage. Among the four aircraft still in service, 4X-ECF was under routine maintenance leaving three with r/c 4X-ECB, 4X-ECD and 4X-ECE airworthy.

4X-ECA, the first El Al Boeing 777-258ER landing at Heathrow Airport on 22 March 2015. (Lewis Grant)

4X-ECD, the fourth Boeing 777-258ER is taking off from Charles de Gaulle Airport on 2 August 2023. (Babak Taghvaee)

4X-ECE, a Boeing 777-258ER taking off from Charles de Gaulle Airport on 9 August 2023. (Babak Taghvaee)

In October 2023, 4X-ECB was spotted flying to Bangkok, Dubai, Moscow, New York and Phuket; 4X-ECD flew to Athens, Bangkok, Milan, Moscow and Phuket, while 4X-ECE flew to Athens, Amsterdam, Bangkok, Istanbul, London and Paris. Following the closure of the Israeli embassy in Ankara and consulate in Istanbul due to the threat of terrorist attacks in Turkey, 4X-ECE was flown to Istanbul to evacuate Israeli diplomats and their families on 20 October. The three 777-258ERs were used to repatriate thousands of Israeli Defence Force reservists to take part in Operation *Iron Swords* from 8–18 October 2023.

El Al also operated a Boeing 777-28ER owned by ILFC under a short-term dry-leasing contract from 3 January to 2 June 2016. The aircraft with r/c EC-MIA (c/n 28685) was built in 2002 and had two Pratt & Whitney PW4090 turbofans.

The Boeing 777-258ERs each had seating configurations for 279 passengers in four classes. Six in first class, 35 in business class, 34 in premium economy class and 204 in economy. 4X-ECE, which had its cabin interior upgraded, had passenger seatings for 313 people (28 business class seats, 32 premium economy seats and 253 economy seats).

Boeing 787-858/958: 2017–Today

By 2005, 12 El Al Boeing 747s and 767s had reached an average age of 20 years. Their increased life, alongside their high number of flying hours and cycles increased their maintenance and operation costs. El Al subsequently began reviewing a replacement for them. The airline chose Boeing 787 Dreamliner and signed agreements with Boeing Commercial and several aircraft lessors to secure 16 brand new aircraft. Of these, 12 would be the 787-9 variant and four the shorter Model 787-8 variant.

The cost of these aircraft, their engines, spare part support, maintenance support and crew training was US$1.25bn making it the largest aircraft procurement programme of in El Al's history. In February 2016, El Al contracted Rolls-Royce to purchase Trent 1000 turbofan engines for the Boeing 787s. The 16 Boeing 787-8/9s were going to replace seven Boeing 747-412/458s and seven Boeing 767-300 series aircraft in service with El Al as of 2016.

The Boeing 787 dates back to the late 1990s when Boeing began designing, developing and building a replacement for the Boeing 767s and Boeing 747-400s. While the Boeing 747-8 was designed as a replacement for Boeing 747-400 series aircraft, the Boeing 787 was designed and developed as a replacement for the Boeing 767. On 16 December 2003, Boeing announced that the 787 would be assembled in its factory in Everett, Washington. The company sub-contracted assemblies including the wing and centre wing box to Japan; horizontal stabilisers to Italy and South Korea; fuselage sections to Italy and the US; passenger doors to France; cargo doors, access doors and crew escape doors to Sweden; software development and floor beams to India; wiring to France; wingtips, flap supporting fairings, wheel well bulkhead and longerons to South Korea; landing gears to France and the UK; and power distribution as well as management systems and air condition packs in the US.

Production of the components for the first prototype started in 2007. It was completed two years later and flew on 15 December 2009. On 26 October 2011, its first customer, All Nippon Airways, received the first Boeing 787. United Airlines, Japan Airlines and American Airlines were the next to receive their aircraft. As of September 2023, a total of 1,087 Boeing 787s in four variants of -8, -9, -10 and Boeing Business Jet (BBJ) were manufactured and delivered to various customers around the world.

After six months of service with the ANA, the Rolls-Royce powered Boeing 787s proved to burn 21 per cent less fuel than the Boeing 767-300ER series. The aircraft's operating cost per seat was 6 per cent lower than the Airbus A330, a twin-engine wide-body airliner with similar size. Its modern aerodynamic design and avionic systems, its lightweight structural parts, of which 80 per cent are made of composite materials, made the aircraft efficient.

Boeing listed the materials used in the Boeing 787 by weight as 50 per cent composite, 20 per cent aluminium, 15 per cent titanium, 10 per cent steel, and 5 per cent other. Aluminium was used throughout the leading edges of wings and tailplanes; titanium is predominantly present within the engines and fasteners, while various individual components are composed of steel. The 787 is the first commercial aircraft to have the majority of its airframe made of carbon fibre reinforced polymer (CFRP), specifically for the empennage, fuselage, wings and doors.

Deliveries and Operations

El Al's order for four Boeing 787-8s and 12 Boeing 787-9s were all delivered as Boeing 787-858s and -958s. The Boeing 787-9s each had seats for 271 passengers including 32 business class, 35 premium economy and 204 economy class, while the Boeing 787-8s had seats for 235 passengers including 20 business class, 35 premium economy and 180 economy seats.

The first two Boeing 787-9s with c/n 63548 and 42117 were built in 2017. They were delivered to El Al on 22 August and 2 October 2017 under a leasing contract with Air Lease Corporation. They received r/c 4X-EDA and 4X-EDB and were named *Ashdod* and *Rishon LeZion*.

In 2018, Boeing manufactured six more Boeing 787-9s for El Al with c/n 38086, 63392, 63393, 63394, 38085 and 38800. They received r/c 4X-EDC, 4X-EDD, 4X-EDE, 4X-EDF, 4X-EDH and 4X-EDI and

4X-ERA, one of the four El Al Boeing 787-858s is at Charles de Gaulle Airport on 22 August 2023. (Babak Taghvaee)

Tel Aviv-Jaffa, *Haifa*, *Bat Yam*, *Rehovot*, *Be'er Sheva* and *Herzliya* fleet names, respectively. They were delivered on 21 February, 1 March 2018, 27 June, 19 August and 29 October 2018 and 14 January 2019, respectively.

In 2019, El Al received four more Boeing 787-958s with c/n 65086, 63395, 65094 and 38783, as well as the first two Boeing 787-858s with c/n 63396 and 63397. They were delivered on 2 April, 18 June, 11 July, 17 September, 27 November and 18 December 2019, respectively. They received r/c 4X-EDJ, 4X-EDK, 4X-EDL, 4X-EDM, 4X-ERA and 4X-ERB and *Kfar Saba*, *Eilat*, *Akko*, *Jerusalem of Gold*, *Ramat Ha Sharon* and *Hod Ha Sharon* fleet names.

In 2020, Boeing completed the manufacture of two Boeing 787-858s with c/n 63398 and 63399. They received r/c 4X-ERD and 4X-ERC, respectively, and *Nof Hagalil* and *Daliat El Carmel* fleet names. They were delivered on 20 February 2020 and 23 July 2023. Both of these aircraft are owned by El Al today.

Today, four Boeing 787-858s and four Boeing 787-958s are owned by El Al, while eight other Boeing 787-958s are operated under long-term leasing contracts with Aviation Capital Group (4X-EDC and 4X-EDH), AerCap Holdings NV (4X-EDI, 4X-EDJ, 4X-EDL and 4X-EDM) and Air Lease Corporation (4X-EDA and 4X-EDB).

In October 2023, when this book was written, the four Boeing 787-858s were flying to Amsterdam, Athens, Bangkok, Boston, Bucharest, Dubai, Fort Lauderdale, Johannesburg, Larnaca, Miami, New York, Pafos, Paris, Rome and Tokyo, while the 12 Boeing 787-958s were flying to Amsterdam, Athens, Bangkok, Dubai, Paris, Larnaca, London, Los Angeles, Miami, New York, Rome and Tokyo.

On 12 October 2023, Boeing 787-958 with r/c 4X-EDC flew to Istanbul to repatriate several Israeli citizens from Turkey.

4X-ERA is in Paris on 22 August 2023. (Babak Taghvaee)

4X-ERC, an El Al Boeing 787-858 landing at Charles de Gaulle Airport in August 2023. (Babak Taghvaee)

El Al's 787-958 with r/c 4X-EDD received this special livery for new flights to Las Vegas and San Francisco in 2019. (Brian Griffin)

4X-EDD, a Boeing 787-958, has landed at Charles de Gaulle Airport. (Babak Taghvaee)

Boeing 787-958 with r/c 4X-EDE after landing at Charles de Gaulle Airport in August 2023. (Babak Taghvaee)

4X-EDF, an El Al Boeing 787-958 is the sole aircraft in retro colours. (Babak Taghvaee)

4X-EDI, is one of 12 Boeing 787-958s in use by El Al. It belongs to AerCap Holdings NV and is being operated under a long-term leasing contract. (Babak Taghvaee)

4X-EDL is another Boeing 787-958s of AerCap Holdings NV leased by El Al. (Babak Taghvaee)

Rolls-Royce Trent 1000 turbofan engines on El Al's Boeing 787-958s each produce 71,000lbf (320kN) thrust. This image shows the left engine of 4X-EDL. (Babak Taghvaee)

Currently, eight of the 12 Boeing 787-958s in use with El Al are leased from aircraft leasing companies including 4X-EDM, which is one of four leased from AerCap Holdings NV. It is at Charles de Gaulle Airport in August 2023. (Babak Taghvaee)

El Al's retro livery of 4X-EDF. (Steve Jones)

Appendix 1

Incidents and Accidents

Thirteen El Al aircraft have faced major incidents and accidents. Of these, six have been fatal. The deadliest occurred to a Lockheed L-149, near Petrich, Bulgaria, on 27 July 1955, when 58 passengers and crew perished after it was shot down by a Bulgarian Air Force MiG-15 fighter. El Al's aircraft have been the target of Palestinian terrorists since the early 1960s.

13 June 1949
An unknown C-47 leased by El Al made a crash landing near Kolunda, Israel. The two pilots and eight passengers were unharmed.

5 February 1950
A Douglas C-54A-10-DC r/c 4X-ACD with four crew members and 46 passengers on board was seriously damaged and caught fire after it skidded off the runway during take-off from Lod Airport, Tel Aviv.

24 November 1951
4X-ADN, a C-54B-1-DC of El Al which previously had r/c 4X-ADB, crashed into a forest between the villages of Winkel and Rüti while on approach to Zürich-Kloten Airport, Switzerland. The aircraft was carrying textiles as cargo to Amsterdam. The six crew members and seven passengers on board all lost their lives. It crashed due to low visibility around Zürich where the aircraft was going to have a refuelling stop.

27 July 1955
A Lockheed L-149 Constellation with r/c 4X-AKC on a flight from Tel Aviv to London with seven crew and 51 passengers on board was shot down by a Bulgarian Air Force MiG-15 after it deviated from its route and strayed into Bulgarian airspace. There were no survivors.

23 July 1968
El Al flight LY426, a Boeing 707-458 r/c 4X-ATA en route to Tel Aviv and carrying 10 crew and 41 passengers was hijacked by three men from the PFLP terrorist organisation. The aircraft was flown to Algiers Dar el Beida Airport, where it remained until 31 August 1968. All of the crew and passengers on board were released in exchange for 16 convicted Arab prisoners.

26 December 1968
Two terrorists belonging to the Popular Front for the Liberation of Palestine used sub-machine guns and a grenade to attack 4X-ATR, a Boeing 707-358B carrying 11 crew and 40 passengers on board at Athens Ellinikon International Airport, while it was taxiing prior to take-off. They killed a passenger and seriously injured a flight attendant. The aircraft was later repaired and flown back to Tel Aviv.

18 February 1969
El Al Flight LY432 from Zürich to Tel Aviv carrying 11 crew and 17 passengers was attacked by four terrorists belonging to the Popular Front for the Liberation of Palestine. The aircraft was attacked when it was taxiing before departure. Attackers sprayed the aircraft with bullets resulting in serious injuries to the co-pilot Yoram Peres, who died of his injuries. An Israeli security guard on board named Mordechai Rahamim returned fire at the terrorists and killed one of them. The aircraft was repaired and returned to Tel Aviv.

6 September 1970
A Boeing 707-458 carrying 10 crew and 138 passengers from Tel Aviv to New York via Amsterdam was hijacked by two Palestinian terrorists including Leila Khaled. One of the terrorists was shot dead by an El Al security guard, while Khaled was overpowered. The aircraft made an emergency landing at Heathrow Airport.

16 August 1972
4X-ATT, a Boeing 707-358C with eight crew members and 140 passengers on board was damaged when an explosive device detonated in its aft baggage compartment ten minutes after take-off from Rome's Fiumicino Airport on a flight to Tel Aviv. The aircraft was flying at 14,500ft over the Mediterranean Sea when the explosion occurred. Pilots immediately declared an emergency and returned to Rome. The aircraft was repaired and returned to service.

31 July 1980
The rear lavatory of 4X-ATX, a Boeing 707-358C, caught fire immediately before a flight. All crew and passengers on board were evacuated. Ben Gurion Airport's fire department put out the fire after cutting a hole in the fuselage. 4X-ATX was repaired and returned to service. It was flown until 1989 when it was put into storage and then sold to IAI in 1992.

4 October 1992
The second deadliest crash of an El Al aircraft took place at Amsterdam when El Al flight 1862 from JFK Airport to Amsterdam crashed into the city. The Boeing 747-258F cargo aircraft had three crew and one passenger on board. The accident occurred after fatigue of the inboard mid-spar fuse-pin connecting the pylon of the number three Pratt & Whitney JT9D-7J engine to the wing of the aircraft broke resulting in the separation of the engine. The separating engine also tore off the fourth engine under the right wing. The crew declared an emergency and while they were about to land, lost control. The aircraft stalled and collided with an 11-story building killing the four people on board and 39 people inside the building.

17 November 2002
The air marshal onboard flight LY581 from Tel Aviv to Istanbul prevented a passenger from hijacking the aircraft. The aircraft landed safely in Istanbul and the passenger was handed over to the police.

28 March 2018
Boeing 767-3Q8ER with r/c 4X-EAK was seriously damaged due to a ground collision with a Boeing 737-76J(WL) at Ben Gurion Airport. The structural damage was too expensive to repair resulting in the withdrawal of the aircraft from service.

Appendix 2
El Al's Fleet Details

Fleet in October 2023

Aircraft Type	Owned	Leased	On order
Boeing 737-804/858/85P/86n/8BK/8HX/86Q/8Q8/8Z9	6	10	-
Boeing 737-958ER	8	0	-
Boeing 777-228ER	6	0	-
Boeing 787-858	4	0	-
Boeing 787-958	4	8	-
Total	28	18	-

Historic Fleet (including subsidiary airline, Sun D'Or International)

Aircraft type	Total number used	Introduced	Last removed from fleet
C-46A/D Commando	8	1948	1956
C-47-DL Dakota	1	1951	1952
C-54A/B Skymaster	7	1948	1952
Lockheed L-149 Constellation	6	1950	1962
Bristol 175 Britannia	5	1957	1967
Boeing 707-138B/139B	2*	1978	1982
Boeing 707-321/323B/328B/329/349C/358B/358C/373C	14	1966	1992
Boeing 707-441/458	4	1960	1986
Boeing 720-058B	2	1962	1980
Boeing 737-2M8/258 Advanced	4	1980	2000
Boeing 737-758	2	1999	2016
Boeing 747-123(SF)/124(SF)/131/132(SF)	5	1977	1999
Boeing 747-2B5BF/228F/238B/245F/258B/258BM/258C/258F/273C	13	1971	2011
Boeing 747-341	1**	2000	2000

Aircraft type	Total number used	Introduced	Last removed from fleet
Boeing 747-412/412F/419/458	9	1994	2019
Boeing 757-23A/27B(ET)/236(ET)/258/258(ET)	13	1987	2012
Boeing 767-258(ER)/27E(ER)	6	1983	2013
Boeing 767-3Q8(ER)/33A(ER)/3Y0(ER)/330(ER)/352(ER)	7	2004	2019

* Chartered
** Wet-leased

Other books you might like:

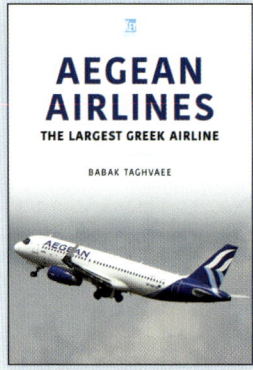

Airlines Series,
Vol. 17

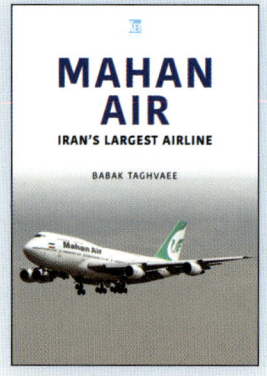

Airlines Series,
Vol. 13

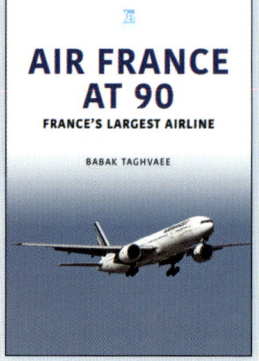

Airlines Series,
Vol. 18

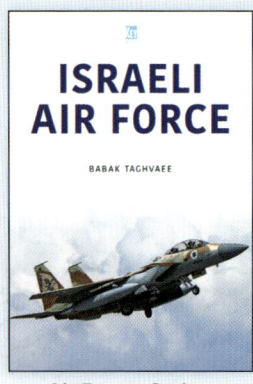

Air Forces Series,
Vol. 10

Air Forces Series,
Vol. 11

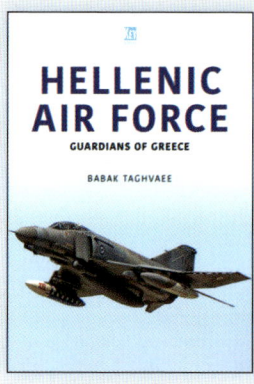

Air Forces Series,
Vol. 8

For our full range of titles please visit:
shop.keypublishing.com/books

VIP Book Club

Sign up today and receive
TWO FREE E-BOOKS

Be the first to find out about our forthcoming
book releases and receive exclusive offers.

Register now at **keypublishing.com/vip-book-club**

*Our VIP Book Club is a 100% spam-free zone, and we will never share your email with anyone else.
You can read our full privacy policy at: privacy.keypublishing.com*